# You Are Here

Discover Better Relationships by
Learning the Language of Emotion

Bryan T. Duncan, PhD & Susan C. Duncan, PhD

*You Are Here*
© 2024 by Bryan and Susan Duncan
All rights reserved. No part of this publication may be reproduced in any form or by any electronic or mechanical means, including information storage and retrieval systems, without permission in writing by the publisher, except by a reviewer who may quote brief passages in a review. For information regarding permission, contact the publisher at info@dacounseling.com.

> This book is available at special discounts when purchased in quantity for use as premiums, promotions, fundraisers, or for educational purposes. For inquiries and details, contact the author at info@dacounseling.com.

Published by Courageous Heart Press
College Station, Texas

Editing and Design by My Writers' Connection

Scriptures marked (ESV) are taken from The Holy Bible, English Standard Version (ESV): Copyright© 2001 by Crossway, a publishing ministry of Good News Publishers. Used by permission.

Scriptures marked (NIV) taken from the Holy Bible, New International Version®, NIV®. Copyright © 1973, 1978, 1984, 2011 by Biblica, Inc.™ Used by permission of Zondervan. All rights reserved worldwide.zondervan.com The "NIV" and "New International Version" are trademarks registered in the United States Patent and Trademark Office by Biblica, Inc.™

Scripture quotations marked (NLT) are taken from the *Holy Bible*, New Living Translation, copyright ©1996, 2004, 2015 by Tyndale House Foundation. Used by permission of Tyndale House Publishers, Carol Stream, Illinois 60188. All rights reserved.

Library of Congress Control Number: 2024941178
Hard Cover: ISBN: 978-1-950714-35-3
Paperback ISBN: 978-1-950714-37-7
Ebook ISBN: 978-1-950714-36-0

# Praise for *You Are Here*

"As a recovering emotional avoider, I found *You Are Here* by Bryan and Susan Duncan to be a valuable tool in my growth toward a healthy way of identifying and expressing my feelings. My family of origin provided an extremely fun, positive, and encouraging environment. The focus in my childhood home was strongly on the good and positive things in life. Because of this, however, negative emotions were never expressed, and I now see that I entered adulthood emotionally unequipped.

"I remember as a newlywed, being asked by my wife, 'How was your day?' and feeling surprised by my realization that she wanted much more than a simple 'Fine.' I began to understand how truly at a loss I was to find words that would accurately express what I was feeling. My inability to relate to the wide range of emotions I experienced myself or saw in others complicated my desire for relational intimacy.

"In *You Are Here*, I learned why having the aptitude to understand and express emotions is so important to our wellbeing and necessary for emotional intimacy with others. The Feeling Grid is a tool I still keep visible on my refrigerator door and refer to often. I especially appreciate the book's reassurance that no feelings are bad; in fact, sometimes the most painful emotions lead us to find the help we desperately need. I am personally grateful to the Duncans for their work and their desire to help us all find the words and the courage to express the emotions God created us to feel."

—**Kelly Davidson**, pastoral care minister, A&M Church of Christ

"As a clinical psychologist, I am often looking for novel ways to help my clients connect with themselves, their emotions, and the other people in their lives. I frequently talk about how the language we use is important, so I particularly enjoyed the way the Feeling Grid breaks down the concept of emotion into six primary emotions that all people experience.

"Bryan and Susan Duncan skillfully guide readers through the process of better defining inner emotional experiences by exploring the ways in which emotions are expressed. I appreciated the definitions of each feeling at the end of each primary emotion chapter. *You Are Here* provides a strong foundation for helping you and your clients identify what they are experiencing emotionally. During a time when people seem more disconnected than ever, I recommend this book for anyone who struggles to pinpoint how they are feeling."

—**Kimberlee DeRushia,** PsyD, licensed clinical psychologist

"In *You are Here*, Bryan and Susan Duncan created a valuable resource for anyone seeking to grow in their emotional intelligence. This book does an excellent job of explaining how emotions serve us and how to better understand their impact on our lives and relationships.

"I found the chapter on anger particularly helpful in understanding how our emotions affect our behavior and interactions with other people. I love the correctives around talking about our sadness and appreciate how the Duncans give permission and encouragement to talk about sadness, so it doesn't morph into anger.

"The definitions and examples of emotions at the end of each chapter are also especially helpful. I suggest using them along with the Feeling Grid. Additionally, there is so much hope and wisdom in the chapter on Joy! The goal of therapy (self or guided) is moving to the right side of the Feeling Grid! We all desire to be joyful, empowered, and peaceful. *You Are Here* and the Feeling Grid are resources that I look forward to using at my therapy practice and sharing with my colleagues and clients."

—**Rev. Dr. Eric J. Liles,** Episcopal priest, licensed professional counselor

"Dr. Bryan Duncan's counsel and relying upon the Feeling Grid were instrumental in my ability to cope with a very difficult situation. Digging into a real understanding of what was driving my feelings changed how I coped and communicated. *You Are Here* is a fascinating, quick read that will impact your life for the better."

—**Kathy M.,** former client

# CONTENTS

| | | |
|---|---|---|
| Foreword | | xi |
| Learning to Feel | | 1 |
| Chapter 1 | The Need for Emotion | 9 |
| Chapter 2 | The Language of Emotion | 27 |
| Chapter 3 | The Feeling Grid | 41 |
| Chapter 4 | Anger | 57 |
| | *Anger Emotions* | 78 |
| Chapter 5 | Sadness | 91 |
| | *Sad Emotions* | 104 |
| Chapter 6 | Fear | 121 |
| | *Fear Emotions* | 138 |
| Chapter 7 | Joy | 153 |
| | *Joy Emotions* | 167 |
| Chapter 8 | Peaceful | 179 |
| | *Peaceful Emotions* | 191 |
| Chapter 9 | Empowered | 205 |
| | *Empowered Emotions* | 219 |
| Chapter 10 | What now? | 235 |
| Appendix | | 241 |
| Bibliography | | 247 |
| About the Authors | | 252 |

To James and Isabel, who inspire us to feel.
(See, we really were writing a book!)

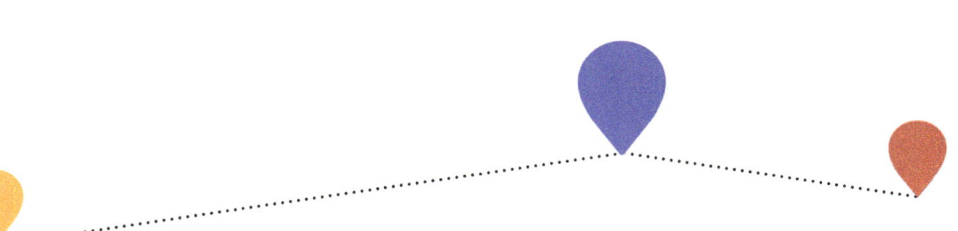

THANK YOU.

To the many clients who have passed through our practice: You have given us a platform to teach and counsel through emotional difficulties. Each of you has been instrumental in the way we have developed, understood, taught, and believed in the power of the Feeling Grid. Some of you listened begrudgingly, but it only helped to build our confidence in what works through that challenge. If we have introduced the Feeling Grid to you, then a part of you is in this book. We hope and pray that future clients can continue to be our source of knowledge about feelings throughout the future.

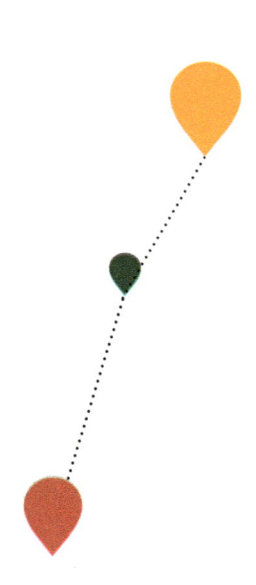

# Foreword

Suffering with post-traumatic stress disorder (PTSD) as a law enforcement professional in the twenty-first century is not easy, even with great strides made in recent decades relative to understanding and treating the disease. I know. I suffered severely from PTSD most of my career in the Drug Enforcement Administration (DEA), which spanned from the late 1960s to the early 2000s.

It was a time of harrowing experiences for those in law enforcement and the military around the globe. I worked undercover against violent drug cartels in cities across the country and served as a DEA attaché in a foreign country, where my survival depended on quickly learning the culture and language. I developed PTSD after a violent, traumatic event early in my career, and further incidents throughout the years amplified the symptoms.

Life progressed, and after many years and numerous stops on the career ladder, I rose through the ranks to become the head of the DEA, a role that had, until then, been held by presidential political appointees from outside the agency. Because of my inside perspective of the danger and essential nature of our work, I was acutely aware of the responsibility that came with being the DEA Administrator. I was accountable for the safety of thousands of people. Beyond the weight of that reality, overseeing a complex multi-billion-dollar agency meant dealing with political, social, budget, and countless other issues, all in the highly charged political atmosphere inside the Washington, D.C. Beltway.

Life was crazy, and much of the time, I felt like I was as well. Most of those years, PTSD had the upper hand. Dealing with the symptoms and effects—guilt, paranoia, anger, alcohol abuse, reckless behavior, even suicidal thoughts—required mental and physical energy and what often felt like futile effort.

Attempting to avoid any stigma, I tried to see a counselor on the sly. I enrolled in the employee assistance program but worried I would somehow be exposed, so I went in for marriage counseling rather than addressing the real issue. That seemed pretty safe; if anyone discovered I was seeing a counselor, I could claim the excuse of my "crazy wife." Still, none of it helped more than just nibbling around the edges of the symptoms and enabling me to somewhat maintain my sanity.

When I retired from the DEA in 2001, the PTSD symptoms didn't fade as I had hoped they would. Instead, they intensified. Again, I tried to just deal with it, but things only got worse with time.

Finally, about seventeen years into my retirement, I found my second chance at life through Drs. Susan and Bryan Duncan. With an intensifying array of PTSD symptoms and a failing marriage, I decided to try counseling again, even though I had little confidence it would help.

After just a couple of sessions, I could see the value of identifying emotions, say fear or anger, and acknowledging how those emotions might relate to feelings of guilt or sadness or could even shift to empowerment. Understanding these connections has enabled me to chart my course through the emotional morass of PTSD.

Life is still not without its struggles, but PTSD no longer rules my existence as it once did. Being able to identify and understand my emotions has made a profound difference in my relationship with my wife as well. After years of neglect, our marriage is recovering and improving every day.

The theory of emotion that Drs. Susan and Bryan Duncan developed and continue to use in their practice with the Feeling Grid, gave me back my life. I know that this book and the understanding it offers can do the same for others from all walks of life and with all kinds of struggles. Of course, my hope is that PTSD sufferers, especially those in law enforcement, will use this book and the Feeling Grid to experience the same freedom I have found.

You do not need to wait thirty years to empower yourself.

**Donnie R. Marshall**
Administrator (Retired)
US Drug Enforcement Administration

# Learning to Feel

**ODDS ARE, NO ONE TAUGHT YOU HOW TO FEEL.** You probably didn't take a class in school on how to identify your feelings. And if you are like a lot of people, no one gave you a lesson on the topic of communicating and connecting through emotion. In fact, if anyone taught you anything about dealing with emotions, chances are good that it was to stuff those feelings away and pretend like everything was fine.

In counseling, one question on the intake form for a new client is, "Did the individual meet all developmental milestones?" The Centers for Disease Control (CDC) summarizes developmental milestones as "From birth to five years, your child should reach milestones in how he or she plays, learns, speaks, acts and moves."[1] The CDC even has a mobile app so new parents can track their child's milestones. When a seventy-year-old man comes to my office because he needs to work on getting along with his wife of forty-nine years, I pause at this question and chuckle. I want to add a feeling milestone with the question, "Did the individual learn how to feel as a child?" The CDC doesn't list *learning to feel* as a developmental milestone. Maybe that's why almost every client who visits our office comes with a lack of emotional knowledge. They feel; they just don't know what to do with their emotions. Put another way, they don't know *how* to feel.

What do you do when you don't know how to express yourself? If you're like most of the clients my wife and I see in our practice, you get angry.

## HOW DOES THAT MAKE YOU FEEL?

*Everyone* feels, but we don't always share or express those feelings.

When I began working as a psychologist in 2007, client after client struggled to answer the infamous question, "So, how does that make you feel?" It seemed like nobody really knew, which was the reason they ended up on my couch.

I noticed, however, that as clients learned to recognize their feelings and how to connect with other people through their emotions, their presenting problems diminished. Anxiety, panic attacks, loneliness, depression, obsessiveness, and relational issues all became less of a factor in their daily lives. After seeing this incredible change in my clients' lives, helping people gain an understanding of emotion became my career passion and quest.

Learning how to recognize, understand, and verbalize emotions *is* ~~like~~ learning a new language. When we're studying a new language, be it Spanish, French, or Mandarin, we often rely on tools (think flash cards, audio programs, books, and apps) to teach and remind us about the essential rules of the language. That's why I created the Feeling Grid. (It's also why Susan and I are writing this book.)

The Feeling Grid is a tool that equips people to communicate with emotion. It gives you the language to better understand and verbally express how you feel, and it teaches you to recognize others' emotions and connect with people through the feelings they share.

## EVOLUTION OF THE FEELING GRID

The first time I used a tool that focused on emotion, I was a predoctoral intern at Appalachian State University's Counseling and Psychological

Services Center. A fellow intern handed me the Feeling Wheel and flippantly said, "Here you go. Have fun with this in session."[2] Picture a Trivial Pursuit game piece full of different-colored pie pieces, with a feeling written on each piece: sad, mad, tired, happy, embarrassed. As a brand-new psychologist, I was already fighting off my impostor syndrome of, *Am I really good at this*, so I threw the colorful tool into a drawer.

A year later, after taking a job as a full-fledged psychologist at a university, impostor syndrome conquered, I came across the folder as I was preparing for my first group therapy meeting. I thought, *Eh, I could probably use this as a fun tool to break the ice.*

It worked—sort of. What worked was my realizing people couldn't pinpoint or talk about their feelings as freely or insightfully as I thought they would be able to do. The tool helped some clients identify possible feelings, but most had a hard time finding a word that worked for them. Likewise, I even struggled to accurately predict what the client would choose. We made progress in our sessions, but the needle of emotional awareness did not really move. A tool was definitely needed to learn about emotion.

I needed a better tool.

The original wheel listed seventy-eight feelings, with six basic emotions in the middle. As I adapted this tool for my practice, the wheel expanded. Eight years into my career, the wheel still had six basic emotions, but it included 114 feelings. The preciseness of the feeling words made it easier for clients to connect emotionally with themselves and made it easier for me to predict more accurately what they were feeling. Therapeutically, however, I knew something was still missing.

## FEELINGS ARE *LINEAR*

While employed as a staff psychologist in a university setting, I worked with hundreds of clients in both individual sessions and through the group therapy program. After logging 3,000 hours of counseling, I noticed the linear pattern in my clients' emotions. Even when clients struggled to describe how they felt, they could typically find a word that accurately defined how they *wanted to feel*. Revising the tool again, I moved the feeling words around the wheel to sit adjacent to feelings that lined up with one another. Based on client feedback and their attainment of therapeutic goals, the Feeling Wheel kept evolving.

After five years as a staff psychologist, my family relocated to a small town in Texas. My wife, the other Dr. Duncan (Susan), and I established a new private counseling practice. The environment was completely different, and I wondered whether we would see the lack of emotional awareness that I had noticed in my clients on campus. If so, would the emotional linearity be similar for the clients in our new town? Would my evolved feeling tool work with this population? To find out, I walked down to the local copy shop on Main Street, printed off a stack of colorful feeling wheels, and gave them to our new clients.

The answer to both questions was *yes*. The struggle to connect with emotion was the same in our small-town private practice as it had been in a university setting. From college students to middle-aged couples to the eighty-five-year-old farmer, everyone struggled to understand and communicate their emotions.

I wore out those feeling wheels in my sessions as I used the tool to help clients identify how they felt—or how they wanted to feel. Recognizing and learning from the linear connection of emotions became a critical aspect of my practice, which made the layout of the wheel ineffective. While simply talking about emotions and sharing feelings was effective, my clients or I would hit a wall in therapy. I needed to create something that went deeper in my clients' therapeutic journey. Letting go of the security of that first emotional tool, I decided to trust my decade and a half of experience and skills and started from scratch.

Focusing on the concept of the linearity of feelings, I developed the Feeling Grid. I liked the grid format, but the real test would be to introduce it to my clients. Some of my clients had been using the wheel for months, so I knew their ability to make the shift would be telling.

They loved it! The specificity of the feeling words and their intentional placement on the grid made it easy to use *and* allowed for a deeper understanding of the linear nature of emotion.

A couple of years after we established our private counseling practice, Susan began collaborating alongside my work and helped to further develop the Feeling Grid. As she used the Feeling Grid with her clients, her insight proved essential. Through our experiences with clients, feedback, and discussion, the Feeling Grid has continued to evolve.

As clients learned to identify emotions more effectively, we made an interesting observation: When people learn how to recognize and accurately identify their feelings, they stop relying on anger as their go-to expression of emotion. Conversely, when clients could not identify their emotion, anger remained the primary way of interacting. Clients either developed their emotional knowledge or they stayed angry.

> *When people learn how to recognize and accurately identify their feelings, they stop relying on anger as their go-to expression of emotion.*

The Feeling Grid develops and enhances people's ability to connect emotionally, which improves communication and leads to deeper, longer-lasting relationships. It created a huge shift in our practice, and we continue to use the tool with our clients. Today, we incorporate the

Feeling Grid into all parts of our practice, including marital intensives, organization workshops, leadership training, individual sessions, and group therapy. During the COVID-19 shutdown, we taught a Bible study for our church that focused on the Feeling Grid. We even use the Feeling Grid with our twin teenagers, Isabel and James; in fact, Susan credits the Feeling Grid for helping her develop deeper relationships with each of them. She has noticed that when she shares how she feels in the moment, her frustration decreases, and Isabel and James draw closer to her because they know where she is emotionally—and sometimes respond by sharing their feelings. Her experience, like that of so many of our clients, affirms the power of emotional connection: When we share our feelings, we grow closer.

## WHO SHOULD USE THE FEELING GRID?

For the past seventeen years, I've taught thousands of clients in a variety of settings, from group and individual therapy to marital intensives (The Marriage Knot) to seminars in business settings. Feelings have been at the center of every session and moment of growth. Drawing on what Susan and I have seen and experienced with our clients as they learned a new way to connect with family, friends, and coworkers, we have developed the Feeling Grid as a tool for them, for us—and for you.

Every person who sits on our couch, meets with us over Telehealth, or comes to a seminar or workshop benefits from using the Feeling Grid. Why? Because every person feels, and every diagnosis has an underlying emotional need that needs to be identified and addressed.

So who is the Feeling Grid for?

- It's for mental health professionals who need a tool to help clients develop emotional awareness.
- It's for people who want to repair hurting relationships and connect with others more deeply and effectively.
- It's for anyone who wants to learn how to be a calmer and more confident person.

In short, Susan and I wrote this book for you. We believe that including emotion in your personal and professional relationships will improve your life, and the Feeling Grid is the tool to help you do that.

Emotions are the way we connect with and relate to friends, family members, clients, and coworkers. When you learn to use the Feeling Grid to speak the language of emotion—a language that allows you to recognize, understand, and verbalize your feelings—every relationship in your life benefits, including the one you have with yourself!

Now, how does that make you feel?

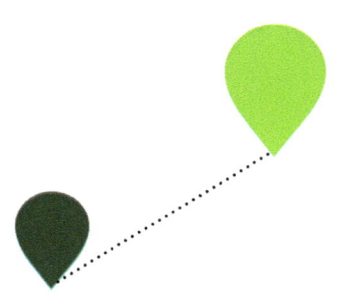

→ 1

# The Need for Emotion

*POWER THROUGH.*
*Suck it up.*
*Never let 'em see you sweat.*
*Quit your crying!*

Humans are emotional beings. For individuals to function in society and for society to function well, emotional connection is essential. Unfortunately, most people try to avoid, diminish, or hide their feelings. Society teaches us early on that emotion is a sign of weakness or immaturity. So instead of learning to understand how to connect through emotion, people learn how to cope. Only, it doesn't work.

Coping behaviors often sound like *suck it up; power through; never let them see you sweat*! When these reactions fail, anger sets in.

We have spent two decades and thousands of hours in session with people who sought therapy because they felt lonely or disconnected. Many clients come to us because they are struggling to save friendships, marriages, and family relationships. We have learned that emotion is the missing link. Emotion is what all humans need in order to connect, but emotion is the very thing most people either do not understand or refuse to acknowledge. Think about it: *How often do you talk about how you are feeling in the moment?*

Leaving emotion out of our everyday interactions is a social and cultural norm on a global scale. It is not working; in fact, it is working against us. Eliminating emotion is why the world is full of *Angerballs*.

Angerballs are people who let their feelings build up inside them and cover up how they really feel by getting mad, shutting down, casting blame, or pointing fingers.

Wait, aren't these *passionate* people sharing their emotions?

No. There is a significant difference between being an Angerball and connecting through emotion. Angerballs are not *sharing* emotion; they are exploding and covering up their emotion. They deny their true feelings and react in anger, clinging to social and cultural norms, like *real men don't cry* or *asking for help is a sign of weakness*. Most people who become Angerballs, which is all of us, actually become more disconnected from those around them.

Relationships—be it work, friend, romantic, or family relationships—are disconnected when true emotion gets eliminated and is replaced with anger. Even as technology has made the world seem smaller by expanding opportunities to connect globally, it has also created an emotionally anorexic and isolating way of relating.

Not sharing how we feel in the moment leads to defective communication. If we are not sharing our emotions, we are not communicating effectively, we are not relating to one another, and we certainly aren't connecting. The pervasive belief seems to be that showing emotions and sharing how you feel in the moment is weak, unsuccessful, and damaging. The outcome of this false belief is that sharing one's feelings and using emotion to connect falls somewhere between unimportant and unacceptable.

The truth is that being human means you cannot eliminate emotion from your life. Emotion is essential to your well-being because *you are an emotional being*.

## "DON'T GET EMOTIONAL!"

Humans have an innate need for emotional connection, meaning emotion exists within us from birth. So how did this disdain for emotional sharing originate? Probably more by default than anything else. The most common reason that people hide, deny, and avoid emotions, based on our experience, is fear. When we are afraid, the need to survive kicks in. Most people skip over acknowledging fearful feelings (as you will learn in this book) and go straight to anger as a means of survival.

Historically, humans have focused their energy on survival. That was true thousands of years ago, but it is also true of our more recent history. Think about it: Generation after generation has had to struggle for survival, from the Great Depression to wars (World War I, World War II, the Korean War, and Vietnam) to the fight for civil rights and social justice. Whether it was fighting as a group or individually, for the majority of the time, emotions were (and are) excluded from the equation.

The introduction of social media did not help emotion get back on the relational map either! Now, the world is busy reacting to one another's comments or opinions. Talking face-to-face about emotions in the moment is difficult enough, let alone sitting at a computer staring at something you just read. Odds are you are going to react, not share your feelings.

When I (Susan) was in graduate school, my roommate's brother posted some photos on Facebook. They were artistic, daily life kinds of pictures. The first thing I noticed about the pictures was that there were no people in them. I made a joke about it in a comment on his post. To me, the joke was funny and harmless. My family teased my dad regularly for his pictures that left out whatever we thought was most important, like the time he took pictures of everyone at the baseball game except my brother on the pitcher's mound. My roommate emailed me the next day. I giggled, thinking she was going to tell me how funny her brother thought I was. Instead, she bluntly stated, "My brother was posting pictures to gain confidence in himself, and you made fun of him." I still remember the embarrassment I felt. It got worse when she followed up with a comment about my relationship with my mom and how I needed to reexamine myself.

She was so protective of her brother (which was the only beautiful part of the story). In response, I got protective of *myself* and turned into an Angerball. I deleted her email and never spoke to her again. It seemed easier to shift into survival mode, get mad, and shut down than to admit the embarrassment and sadness I felt for her and her brother. I sure do miss her.

It's important to remember that survival mode is not always bad. Actual war or growing up in an abusive family are just a couple of examples of when survival mode is necessary. The problem is that entire generations were unable to downshift out of survival mode due to war or social injustice, and that is not a sustainable way to live. When you're in survival mode, you have little to no time to pause and process how you feel. Experiencing and sharing emotions can even seem *counterproductive* to survival. Staying in survival mode stunts the growth of emotional connection.

*Staying in survival mode stunts the growth of emotional connection.*

Maybe you've heard or internalized statements that seemed to prove the riskiness of showing emotion:

*Emotions make you look weak.*

*Don't get emotional.*

*I don't have time to slow down and wallow in my feelings.*

*Showing your feelings shows a lack of control.*

*You wear your emotions on your sleeve.*

*Being emotional is just feeling sorry for yourself.*

*I don't want anyone's pity.*

*You're just being sensitive.*

We've heard them all, but we have also seen how staying in survival mode is the impetus to believing these statements and having no ability to express or share emotions. About 95 percent of our clients end up talking about what makes them angry. And 99 percent of *those* clients (a few don't stick around) end up realizing they are experiencing emotions that they have been covering up with anger. The other 5 percent of clients come in for therapy because they realize they have been angry for the past decade (give or take a few) and they are *exhausted*. A few have already figured out that they had been using their anger as a mask to hide their sadness or fear. Having removed the mask of anger, they are flailing amid all the feelings and need guidance on what to do with them.

We wrote *You Are Here* because we believe emotional connection is essential for your well-being. After years of working to help people learn to identify and use their true feelings to connect with others, we know that this skill can improve the quality of your relationships. If you can learn how to decrease the amount of time you feel anger, you can increase your ability to connect through your other emotions.

## THE WRONG KIND OF EMOTIONAL TRAINING

Unlike the instinct to survive, emotional awareness is a learned skill. Unfortunately, most of us are trained how *not* to emote from the very beginning. *Stifling* the awareness of emotions is also a learned skill!

When toddlers fall, parents immediately reassure their children. "It's okay. You are fine. Keep on going." That misdirected reassurance is followed by a pause during which parents hold their breath, hoping their toddler doesn't cry. Parents know that if they display any emotion (fear, for example), the toddler will cry. So parents put on their best poker face or an encouraging grin, hoping to avoid any tearful or loud display of emotion. If their little one's face shows signs of sadness, hurt, or frustration, parents jump into action to divert attention away from anything outside of the happy zone.

It is as if parents don't want two-year-olds to act like babies. Toddlers *are* babies. Babies cry. It's a natural expression of emotion.

From early on, we learn to refrain from showing emotion—how to not get overly excited or to quickly wipe away tears. Remember *A League of Their Own*, and the famous (or infamous) line, "There's no crying in baseball!" Think about it: Would crying tears of joy after a home run have made Babe Ruth any less of a batter? No! For that matter, if our daughter had cried less when she fell off her horse and broke her arm, would that have made her arm less broken? Nope. Telling her not to cry at the pain she felt would have been pointless. (Besides, broken arms hurt!) Did she have to get back on her horse to overcome the fear of falling off again? Yes. But telling her not to be scared or pretending that fear was wrong would not have helped her feel better. Talking through her emotions gave her the confidence to ride again.

We can get so good at not showing emotion that we deny we have felt *anything* at all. This denial has a name: alexithymia. Lori Gottlieb explains this well in her best-selling book, *Maybe You Should Talk to Someone*, while sharing how her client exhibits this emotional blindness: "It's not that she's hiding her feelings; it's that she can't access them. She doesn't know what she is feeling or doesn't have the words to express it."[3]

Consider this hypothetical scenario: Let's say you are on a camping trip with friends. You're all gathered around the campfire when a bear comes out of the woods and approaches the campsite. What do you do? You jump up and run away screaming! (Okay, maybe not if you are an Eagle Scout, but stay with us.)

When survival mode kicks in, you instinctively move into action. You don't sit there by the fire in your cozy camping chair and process how scared you are. Nor do you look over your shoulder as you're running away and shout, "Hey, bear! You are scaring me right now. I am so afraid of your claws and teeth." No, you run until you feel safe.

---

*We can get so good at not showing emotion that we deny we have felt anything at all.*

---

What happens when the bear is gone, and everyone has survived? You start to *feel* a lot of things! But you move on. You focus on everything from how to stay safe the rest of the night to where to put the food so the bear doesn't return—*anything* except that raw emotion created by the experience. Why not talk about the intense fear you felt? Maybe you don't know how to process what you're feeling, or you doubt the other campers were as scared as you. Looking around, it doesn't seem like anyone else wants to talk about it either, so you push the fear to the back of your mind. Basically, you stay in survival mode, refusing to process how you feel and missing out on experiencing emotional connection with others.

Here is another example, maybe more relatable to our every day. I (Susan) was eating lunch with my four-year-old twins. This lunch happened to be in our truck in the parking lot of my office, and both children were sitting in the back in their car seats, unbuckled with a little freedom to move about. I glanced back as we settled into eating, and James was sitting quietly in his car seat with his food. Half a minute later, I asked if they liked their lunch. James did not answer. I turned to face him and saw that he *couldn't* answer. The engine was off, but my son must have rolled down the window before I turned it off. He had somehow leaned on the window button and rolled the window up on his neck. As my adrenaline surged, I turned the ignition and rolled down the window. He fell back into his car seat, then immediately climbed into the front seat to sit in my lap. I took him in my arms and looked him over. Just as I asked if he was okay, he threw up all over me. I couldn't do anything but hold him while fear-filled questions raced through my mind: *How long? What if?* Then, I shut down my feelings. A few seconds into my mental spiraling, my daughter crawled up beside me, and I held her too.

It was absolutely one of the most terrifying moments of my life. But I just kept going. I did not slow down and feel through any of it! Eventually, I got James and Isabel settled back in their car seats. I stepped out of the truck and removed my vomit-covered jeans right there in the parking lot across from my office. A little less smelly, I climbed in the backseat with both children and smiled and patted their arms, while I called Bryan. He walked over from his office to drive us home. Still, no crying, not even when I explained everything to him once he got in the truck. Later that night, I talked to my brother, a doctor, and told him all about it; I wanted his reassurance that everything was fine—that James would be fine. For me, *fine* was the goal.

Even on the drive home, I remained so focused on surviving and making sure everyone was fine that I didn't stop to ask if my son had been scared or if my daughter, who watched her brother struggle, was sad. In fact, I can't remember how each child felt throughout the experience at all.

We just kept going. *Power through!*

## DEFINING EMOTION

### Emotion

1. a conscious mental reaction . . . experienced as strong feelings usually directed toward a specific object and typically accompanied by physiological and behavioral changes in the body
2. a state of feeling
3. the affective aspect of consciousness: FEELING

*—Merriam-Webster Dictionary*

Based on this definition, emotion doesn't just affect us physiologically and behaviorally; it is part of our consciousness. Emotion allows us to feel—to connect *with* ourselves and *with* others. When we deny or try to ignore emotion, we end up feeling disconnected—*from* ourselves and *from* others. Emotion also helps us understand ourselves and our experiences. Sharing our emotions lets others know where we are and how we are doing in that moment. This is why I cannot remember my son or daughter's reaction on the drive home after our lunchtime scare. I did not slow down and connect emotionally with either of them or their dad! I missed out on connecting emotionally.

## EMOTION EXISTS

If you think you are different because you really are not the type of person who has emotion, you are wrong. Everyone feels and experiences emotion. The definition above states that *emotion is part of our consciousness,* and that means *everyone* experiences emotion. Sometimes emotions are heightened, and sometimes they level off, but they always exist—in everyone.

Think of levels of emotion like degrees in temperature. A temperature of zero does not mean there is no temperature outside. That's because temperature is based on an interval scale, meaning zero is an *absolute* number. Emotion exists even when you think it is not present, just like temperatures that hit zero. Don't you feel something when you walk outside in the snow in shorts?

So, yes, even though you think you are not the type of person who feels, you are experiencing emotion. On the Feeling Grid, one of the feelings is *Numb*, which might resonate with the lack of feeling. But even when you feel numb, you aren't void of emotion. You are still feeling *something*. If you look at the Feeling Grid, you'll see that numb connects to the core emotion of *Sad*.

Emotion is constantly present, even if you are sitting at zero, because emotion is part of your existence. What now?

1. First, recognize the emotion and work to understand it.
2. Use this emotion to connect with yourself and others.

When you follow these steps, over and over again, you are doing something powerful in the world of relating: You are letting others know where you are *emotionally*.

So what exactly does it mean to know where you are emotionally?

## YOU ARE HERE

Let's travel back to 1984 to buy some Yankee candles at the shopping mall. Imagine walking through the giant maze of stores. You pass Colors of Benetton, Orange Julius, Spencer's, and Radio Shack, and then stop. You look around, searching for the Yankee Candle store. You have seen it every time you have walked through the mall, but now you can't remember where it is.

How do you find the store? Do you walk around and yell, "Yankee Candle, where are you?" Do you ask the people walking by if they have seen it? Do you wander up and down each corridor until you find it? Most do all the above, then give up and head back to the mall directory, the map everyone passes on the way into the mall.

Maps are great tools. But they only work if we admit to needing one, preferably before spending forty-five minutes wandering around lost! Back to finding those candles. Once you find Yankee Candle on the list of alphabetized stores, you can find it on the map fairly easily. But, wait.

Knowing the store's location is important, but that information won't do you any good until you know where YOU are. Until you know where you are in the mall, you won't know which direction to turn. To get where you want to go, you need to figure out where you are first. Once you find the You Are Here symbol, you can navigate toward Yankee Candle.

Most people approach relationships like frustrated shoppers who didn't stop to look at the mall directory. They wander around, failing to find what they need. What if the shopper took note of their surroundings when the Yankee Candle seeking began?

Pausing to recognize what you're feeling, why, and maybe even what you want to do with your feelings is like finding the You Are Here symbol on a map. That symbol is not only for your benefit. When you share where you are emotionally, you allow others to connect with you and better understand how to relate to you. Telling someone how you are feeling in the moment helps both you and that person to feel more at ease. That understanding nurtures healthy forward movement in your relationship because neither of you feels lost.

The problem is, most people don't stop to look at the emotional map. Some people are so immersed in survival mode that they can't believe that talking about their emotion would help. Besides that, survival mode has become a way of life. Others don't even know there is a map because they never learned how to feel. In either case, being lost, frustrated, and angry seems normal—or, in other words, *fine*. But is it really fine?

## "I'M FINE." *REALLY?*

We talk about emotions and feelings with every client. While developing the Feeling Grid, Bryan noticed a lack of emotion sharing in his everyday interactions, like at the grocery store or the gas station. I'm *fine*. Everybody can't be fine all the time! We knew everyone wasn't fine because we heard from clients every day, eight hours a day, who were in our offices because they *knew* they were not fine. No one, it seemed, answered the question honestly. While most people consider the question and rote response a formality, we believe robotically responding with, "I'm fine," is a missed opportunity!

## The PDE Plan

Bryan came up with this idea and enacted what I dubbed the Public Display of Emotion (PDE) Plan. This idea started when we were leaving church one day. As our family walked out of service, Bryan observed the greeters shaking hands with members and asking how they were. You could hear every single person in front of us respond, one after the other with, "Fine, thanks." If you go to church on Sunday, you know each of those people was, at the very least, starving. (Church is long and people are hungry!) Bryan decided *fine* was no longer an option.

"You know what?" Bryan said in the car on the way home that day. "From now on, I am going to answer that question truthfully. I hope everyone is ready!" The next time anyone, whether it was the grocery store cashier or a stranger on the street, asked how his day was going, he answered honestly.

"Eh, I have had better days."

"Not great. I just had a fight with my wife."

"Not so bad, but my mom died last year, and today is the anniversary."

After a while, Bryan took his PDE to the next level. When someone answered with an automatic "fine" to his query, he would pause and ask, "But really, are you actually fine?"

Most people didn't know how to respond. Some shrugged. Others stared at him blankly (maybe they had no idea how they were actually feeling). A few came back with in-depth, honest answers.

Pre-PDE Plan, Bryan rarely put himself in uncomfortable social situations, which is one reason it was fun for me to watch this plan play out. Before he understood the power and value of emotional connection, he had been the easygoing, everything-is-fine guy, not the allow-discomfort guy. But the lack of emotional sharing in the world had become obvious, and even more obvious was the emotional disconnect he felt when experiencing the superficial responses. While connecting through emotion in his therapeutic relationships, Bryan came to understand that he needed to use more emotional connection in his everyday life, marriage, parenting, and even grocery shopping. And, as his spouse, I noticed, and I loved it.

I jumped on board with the PDE Plan and began answering honestly and encouraging others to do the same. Think about the typical conversation you have with the cashier at the grocery store. He or she will ask, "How are you today?"

"Fine," you respond. "How about you?"

"I'm fine, thanks for asking."

*Beep*, broccoli . . . *Beep*, crackers . . . *Beep*, milk . . .

"Did you find everything you were looking for?"

"Yes, I did, thanks." (You know that's a lie. Have you ever easily found molasses or breadcrumbs?)

*Beep*, salmon . . . *Beep*, lettuce . . . *Beep*, ice cream . . .

There's no connection between the shopper and the cashier. That must be lonely for the cashier, who endures the same exchange with everyone who passes through the line. No wonder some cashiers seem so bored. They're having the same disinterested conversation a hundred times a day!

I assign the PDE Plan to my clients in therapy. I call it the Grocery Store Cashier assignment. You can try it too. It's simple: When you stop at the grocery store on your way home today, answer honestly when the cashier asks how you are doing.

One of my favorite responses to the introduction of this assignment came from a client whose expression changed dramatically as she visualized the experience. Fear washed over her face, followed by a somewhat stern expression. She sat up straighter, put her shoulders back, and gently moved her hair away from her face. Then she told me there was absolutely no way she could tell the cashier how she was feeling.

In that moment, I realized the acute level of vulnerability some people experience when sharing emotion. Several months into therapy, I asked that client if she had done the Grocery Store Cashier assignment yet. She said she was still working on it. I don't know if she ever completed the assignment, but I hope so.

It's simple and challenging. The growth that can come from even brief emotional connection is worth the few seconds of vulnerability we risk. We experienced that truth as a family one day when we stopped at the grocery store on our way home from the veterinarian's office. We had just put down our dog Flower due to heart failure. We planned a family movie night in honor of Flower's amazing twelve years as our family pet.

---

*The growth that can come from even brief emotional connection is worth the few seconds of vulnerability we risk.*

---

Raw with emotion and still processing our last moments with her, we walked around the store in search of some very unhealthy comfort food.

With our basket loaded with junk food, we entered Lane Two. As usual, the cashier asked, "How are y'all doing today?" (Yes, in the smooth Texas accent you just heard in your head.) I hesitated, glanced back at my kids, and then looked up and said, "We are actually having a really hard day. We just put down our family dog. Now we're buying a bunch of junk food to go home and be sad together while watching a movie." I felt like I owed it to Flower not to dismiss her, even with the cashier at the grocery store.

The cashier paused as she took in what I had gently unloaded onto her. Her face softened. She gently smiled and said, "I am so sorry. That is really sad." With those comforting words hanging between us, she finished scanning and bagging our snacks. As we walked away, she looked up and started to talk, hesitated, and then said, "I hope y'all enjoy the movie together."

In that brief encounter, she experienced some of our sadness with us, and in the end, we all connected. Interestingly, she seemed more lighthearted and alert when we walked away. On the way out, I looked at my family and sighed. "I felt better sharing what we were really doing. It seemed more real." I firmly believe that in my genuineness, I generated a genuine response. There was no superficial "fine." We connected thanks to the PDE Plan!

## Emotions Connect

Learning to recognize and share emotions isn't always easy. But it's worth it. Bryan grew to understand the value of emotional awareness through working with thousands of clients over the years. He had seen it clearly in his clients' progress as they learned the language of emotion. He also benefited from the emotional connection being exchanged in his office with clients.

Please know we are not saying that sharing emotions doesn't feel awkward or uncomfortable at times. The more Bryan practiced, the more he felt connected to his own emotion, which improved his ability to connect to others. Before long, Bryan was sharing emotion more organically than he did at first. He responded one day at the grocery store with, "It has been a really difficult few days. I am trying to make a big decision about my practice, but I'm not sure how it will impact other people. It's getting me down because I worry about what other people think of me. (*Sigh*.) How are you doing?" He admitted to fear, worry, weakness, and sadness all in one breath! He shared his emotions and opened the door for the other person to share and connect on the same level.

Remember that moment the cashier hesitated when I told her why we were buying junk food? I didn't know what was about to happen, but she chose to connect with me and responded with compassion. That connection, which affected my whole family, seemed to bring about a sense of community and even a little hope. A simple exchange of emotion in a moment of sadness or fear allows us to grow together!

## IS YOUR TANK EMPTY?

In *The Soul of Shame*, Curt Thompson equates emotion to the fuel for the human tank. If we remove emotion from the human experience, everything stops. Sharing our true feelings in the moment, however, fills that tank and builds a connection that can make us feel more alive.[4]

So why does something so simple (and so beneficial) seem so difficult? Well, we've already brought up the lack of emotional training and the negative connotations we're taught to believe about showing and sharing emotion. Remember, although emotion exists (it's innate), we must learn the skill of recognizing and communicating our feelings. Meanwhile, culture and society tell us to curb our enthusiasm and that there's no crying—in baseball or anywhere else.

Sometimes, we don't make those emotional connections because we simply don't know *how* we feel. Whether that's true because we're stuck in survival mode or because we've been taught our emotions aren't important, we neglect to stop and check in with our emotions. Other times, we know how we're feeling but don't have the words to express it.

That's why we wrote *You Are Here*. We want to help you experience the power of emotional connection because we believe it is vital. Sharing emotion is what helps us relate to one another. Emotional connection is what fills our souls and fuels our desires. The first step is understanding the reality that emotion exists and is essential to a healthy human experience.

The next step is to learn to recognize *how* you're feeling and how to connect through emotion. Using the Feeling Grid, you'll learn the language of emotion so that the next time someone asks how you are, you'll have the words to give an answer far more honest than, "I'm fine."

Are you ready for your first lesson in the language of emotion?

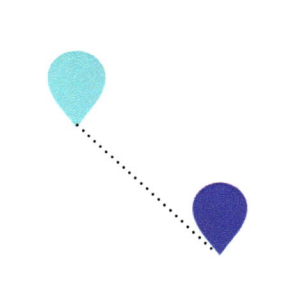

# ② 

# The Language of Emotion

**MISUNDERSTANDINGS ARE NEFARIOUS.** They can ruin a great day in a split second. You say one thing, but your business partner or spouse hears something completely different. Anger ensues, and doors slam. Communication stops, and *dis*connection takes over.

We've all experienced misunderstandings created by words we've used incorrectly or that someone interpreted in a way we did not intend. Before we jump into learning the Feeling Grid, we need to define some terms. Knowing the terminology to use, as well as how and when to express feelings correctly, is an important aspect of learning the nuances of the language of emotion. Terminology matters.

We'll start by looking at a phrase that is misused in our offices every day: *I feel.*

## I FEEL . . .

**Susan**: How do you feel when you walk into the room to see your mom?

**Client**: I feel like hitting my head against the wall!

**Susan**: Okay, understandable, but that's not a feeling.

Putting "I feel" in front of a word does not make that word a feeling. And yet, we hear it all the time:

"I feel like my point is not coming across clearly."

"I feel like we should go the other direction."

"I feel hungry."

"I feel judged by you."

"I feel like I'm hitting my head against the wall."

"I feel . . ."

None of these phrases includes a feeling word. *Judged* is not a feeling. *Hungry* is not a feeling.

This phrase "I feel" has become part of our vernacular, so commonly used that it wouldn't surprise me if it were listed in the dictionary next to *ain't* and *irregardless*. Ain't and irregardless are not actual words but are now in most dictionaries because they have become widely accepted. Misusing terms can create confusion. This is the danger of misusing the term *feel*. Using the words *I feel* does not mean you are stating a feeling.

In therapy and in life, listening for feeling words is one way to better understand others. When someone shares how they are feeling, they are offering a clue to help us understand where they are in the moment or in the relationship. The same thing applies in reverse: When you say, "I feel . . .," the other person learns more about where you are. It is as if they can see the big, red, upside-down teardrop above your head, like on the map in the mall.

When a client follows the phrase *I feel* with anything that is not a feeling, I (therapeutically) interrupt and point out, "That's not a feeling." Then, we work together to find the words that accurately describe how they are feeling. In time, they can replace their non-feeling words with language of emotion—words that clearly describe where they are in the moment.

*I feel like my point is not coming across clearly.* (a belief, not a feeling)
**I am feeling apprehensive** because I don't believe my point is coming across clearly.

*I feel like we should go the other direction.* (a thought, not a feeling)
**I am feeling scared**, and I think we should go the other direction.

*I feel hungry.* (a sensation, not a feeling)
**I am beginning to feel anxious** because my stomach is telling me I am hungry.

*I feel judged by you.* (a fact, not a feeling)
**I feel hurt** by what you are saying because your words seem judgmental.

*I feel like I'm hitting my head against the wall.* (an analogy, not a feeling)
**I am so sad** when I see my mom that it makes me want to hit my head against the wall.

Notice how you immediately understand more about the person? In contrast, when someone uses the *I feel* phrase with non-feeling words, you feel anxious or uneasy because you are not quite sure where they are.

Imagine the emotional connection gained through simple conversation when you start using feeling words. When your friends state that they feel overwhelmed, frightened, appreciated, hopeful, ashamed, or even irritated, you can understand where they are on the map *and* where you are in relation to them.

I feel like you don't understand me.
**I feel embarrassed.**

For Bryan and me, misunderstandings tend to escalate into arguments. He, for example, could tell me that he is going to build something in the garage. If I ask too many questions about the project, he might get frustrated and say, "I feel like you are not understanding anything I say."

Chances are that my reaction to his accusation that I do not understand him would also be one of frustration. "I feel like you are not making any sense."

If, instead, he slowed down and said, "I feel embarrassed that you don't understand what I am explaining to you," he could create the opportunity for an emotional connection, which would head off my reaction of frustration by removing any blame from the situation.

Knowing how someone feels is empowering. It guides you to respond appropriately in the moment. If I misunderstood, for example, "not understanding me" to mean that Bryan felt frustrated rather than embarrassed, my response to his declaration might not have matched his needs.

Using a feeling word with the phrase *I feel* instead of a fact or thought increases the likelihood of an emotional connection. Try it! When you learn to use the language of emotion (feeling words), you will notice that you'll feel more connected to your friends, your spouse, your colleagues, and perhaps even the cashier at the grocery store.

## THE MASQUERADE

In Bryan's junior year of high school, he got a stress fracture in his foot during his cross-country race. It wasn't *worry* that caused the second metatarsal in his right foot to crack; it was physical pressure. The bone had reached its maximum threshold of pressure—and cracked. The realization that Bryan had a stress fracture then caused *him* to become stressed. Overwhelmed with emotion, he went home and exclaimed to his parents, "I am so stressed out about my foot!" Looking back on that memory, he knows what he was really feeling was sadness about missing the rest of the year's cross-country competitions.

It's easy for some words to masquerade as feeling words. Sometimes, these words can act as arrows pointing to an emotion on our map of emotional connection, but they are not feelings or evidence of an emotion.

Similar to the *I feel* phrase, people regularly masquerade their emotion behind words and phrases like these:

"I am stressed out!"

"I just had a panic attack!"

"Oh my gosh, I am about to have an anxiety attack."

"Man, I felt suicidal last night."

The fact that these words and phrases hint at true emotion gives people some measure of comfort, protection from vulnerability (something we will discuss in the Anger chapter), or even a temporary false sense of emotional connection. Additionally, because they elicit an emotional response from the listener, these words serve a purpose in getting other people's attention.

But look at the understanding that we can create by taking off the mask and sharing how we actually feel.

*I am stressed out!* (a sensation, not a feeling)
**I am worried** that I didn't pass my pre-calculus test.

*I just had a panic attack!* (a sensation or reaction, not a feeling)
**I am so frustrated** because I don't have control over this situation.

*Oh my gosh, I am about to have an anxiety attack.* (a sensation or reaction, not a feeling)
**I am dreading** my performance evaluation.

*Man, I felt suicidal last night.* (a description, not a feeling)
Breaking up with her made me **feel worthless and lonely**.

> ## Intense Reaction or Real Connection?
>
> Stress heightens emotions and tends to create bonds between people—even people who have only just met. Remember the movie *Speed*, featuring Sandra Bullock and Keanu Reeves? Their characters, Annie and Jack, wound up on a bus rigged with a bomb. The stress caused by the fear of exploding created a powerful bond between them.
>
> The intense emotion bubbled with a chemistry that made viewers certain Annie and Jack would end up together. He yelled. She yelled. He saved the passengers. She jumped the bus over a giant gap in the freeway. (Yeah, whatever!) They *clicked*!
>
> And then when Jack gives Annie *the look*, she responds by saying, "You're not going to get mushy on me, are you? . . . I hope not, 'cause you know, relationships that start under intense circumstances, they never last."[5]
>
> It's true. Traumatic, stressful, or intense circumstances create a false sense of emotional connection that has the potential to dissolve when the event ends or the credits roll.
>
> Annie's cautious approach is not a bad idea. Time and a little space can help you put an intense interaction in better perspective. Reacting to a scary or traumatic event is not connecting emotionally; it is simply reacting.

The clarity that feeling words bring to the conversation gives us insight and creates an emotional connection. There is no substitute for true feeling words when it comes to connecting emotionally with others.

## Changing the Dynamic with Emotion

The relational dynamic in group therapy illustrates how masquerading emotion is detrimental to success in relationship building. Bryan noticed that when clients got to know one another in group therapy, they typically didn't start by sharing feelings. Instead, people shared details and facts about their lives. That surface-level, fact-based sharing is a normal first step in relationship building, but to build or deepen relationships, it is essential to share true emotion.

Connecting emotionally is necessary in group therapy because of the *Storming* stage of group therapy. Dr. Irvin Yalom, the guru of group therapy, developed the five stages of group: Forming, Storming, Norming, Working, and Adjourning. Yalom defined Storming, Stage 2, this way:

> A transition phase. Anxiety, ambiguity, and conflict become prevalent as group members test and act out behaviors to define themselves and the group norms. This stage creates an interpersonal climate where members should feel free to disagree with each other.[6]

Storming is an *expected* stage in relationship building. The last sentence of the definition points out each person should "feel free to disagree with each other." Don't you agree that's a unique part of relationships? Sharing and discussing jobs, kids, and achievements is one thing, but when your friend goes through a divorce, he or she needs to be able to trust your acceptance and willingness to maintain the friendship. When you lose your job and your buddies want to go out to eat, you want to feel safe with them to admit you can't afford it without feeling rejected. The goal is to *make it through* the Storming stage, not avoid it. The only way to achieve this is by having an emotional connection, to know where your friend is when you share where you are emotionally.

Masquerading in your relationships and telling yourself that you have good connections sets you up for failure when that Storming stage hits.

**Think about your group of friends:**
With whom would you survive the Storming stage?
How do you know? When have you shared emotions?
With which friends do you have emotional connections?

The point of learning to identify masquerading feeling words isn't to avoid them. That would be impossible and, honestly, unnecessary. The goal is to recognize them for what they are—information, sensations, details. Small talk has its purpose, but it does not create the emotional connection needed to make it through feelings of anxiousness or rejection.

## REMOVING THE *EMOTIONAL* LABEL

*I cry too much.*
*I'm too emotional.*
*I am too sensitive.*
*My mom overreacts.*
*My husband is incapable of emotion.*

These are the comments collected over the years in our practice that helped lead to the focus on emotion. People get labeled all the time for too much, not enough, or a void of emotion. If our client is not sitting on our couch because they were told one of these labels of emotion, the client is on the couch labeling their loved one or coworker with it.

When we explore these emotional labels with clients, one thing is consistently true: Neither the client nor the people in their lives who are doing the labeling know how to describe what they are feeling. How do we know? Everything being described within these emotional labels is a reaction, not an emotion.

What does the lack of emotional language skills create?

Angerballs!

Neither the client nor the person the client is talking about has a clue where the other is or where to start on their emotional map to get to the other. The purpose of this book and the Feeling Grid is to equip you with the map you can use until you become fluent in the language of emotion.

## Reactive vs. Emotional

Most emotional labels are not emotions at all. They describe reactions (behaviors). Showing true emotion is the opposite of reacting. Where emotions connect us, reactions tend to have messy consequences. Think about what happens when you combine baking soda and vinegar, thermite and ice, or Mentos and Diet Coke. Just like the mess that's created by these chemical reactions, people who are reactive can create a mess of their relationships—and they may not even realize what they're doing. In the same way the compounds in those experiments just do what they do (react), the people who blow up in anger or dissolve into tears are often doing so without an understanding of what is happening or why.

Worse yet is the mess we make when our reactive behavior is habitual and becomes our label—the way others identify us. Labels stick around. They are difficult to shed. The labels our families give us in childhood often get carried into adulthood. When others expect us to react a certain way, we learn to live up (or down) to that expectation without any knowledge of what we are doing or why. *Knowing where you are* emotionally is essential to mapping out or understanding our reactions.

## FOUR RULES OF COMMUNICATION

It's not uncommon for clients to tell us that sharing emotions doesn't work. We often hear statements like "I've tried telling her how I feel, but she just blows up at me!" or "I told him how I felt, and he stormed out. When he came back, he refused to speak to me."

If you have experienced similar reactions from others, you are not alone. You try to share your feelings only to have your spouse, best friend, child, or coworker react in anger. Then, because anger begets anger (something you'll learn more about in Chapter 4), you get angry right back at them. Rather than finding the connection you had hoped for, you end up feeling more disconnected from that person than you did before you risked sharing your emotions.

It's a destructive cycle that Susan heard repeatedly in counseling sessions. As she listened to her clients' variations of this sharing–anger–more anger cycle, she noticed that there were four things that goaded anger reactions: 1) telling the other person what they were feeling, 2) telling the other person what they were thinking, 3) giving the person unsolicited advice, or 4) making a statement to motivate the other person to give a specific response. Almost without fail, it was when people did one of those four things that they found themselves on the receiving end of an anger reaction.

To circumvent the cycle and to allow emotional sharing to progress, Susan established the Four Rules of Communication:

1) I cannot tell anyone how they feel.
2) I cannot tell anyone what they think.
3) I cannot give anyone advice unless I am asked to give advice.
4) I cannot ask, say, give, or accept anything with motivation.

Break any one of these rules and you'll get an anger reaction.

But if you stick to the rules while sharing what *you* are feeling, you dramatically increase the chances that you'll get a response from the other person, one that includes how they are feeling. Responses can generate growth and emotional connection. They allow the conversation to continue and give the relationship an opportunity to grow.

1. I cannot tell anyone how they feel.
2. I cannot tell anyone what they think.
3. I cannot give anyone advice unless I am asked to give advice.
4. I cannot ask, say, give, or accept anything with motivation.

## What Emotional Really Means

The true definition of what it means to be emotional is to have awareness, knowledge, and understanding of what is causing the feelings of anxiousness, shame, or helplessness. Being emotional—being aware or having knowledge and understanding of ourselves and our feelings—is a good thing. Yes, even if it means you are sad, afraid, or lonely.

In the language of emotion, it's important that we get the terminology right and recognize the distinction between being reactive and being emotional. Likewise, we need to understand that being *emotional* is good!

Everyone experiences emotion. It's when people don't know how they feel that they react. But you don't have to react. You can learn to become emotionally aware and identify your feelings so that rather than creating a mess by reacting, you use your emotion to connect with yourself and others.

## LISTENING: A NECESSARY CATALYST FOR CONNECTING WITH EMOTIONS

Expressions of emotions get missed all the time. Why? Because people don't *listen* for emotions.

People can share their feelings all day long, but if you aren't listening, there will be no emotional connecting or relationship building. Sure, you may hear your spouse, children, or parents, but do you really listen with the intent to understand where the person is emotionally in the moment?

We listen for a living. Our mission is to help the person sitting on the couch across from us, but we cannot do that unless we know where our clients are emotionally. The disdain society has created for showing emotions has taught people how to disguise feelings or use them sparingly. It's the kind of listening Bryan did when living in Cuernavaca, Mexico. He was still learning how to speak Spanish, so to understand what people were saying, he leaned in and focused on their words, their facial expressions, and their body language. That kind of active listening is required for emotional connection.

When we hear someone say, "I feel . . . ," we immediately move to the edge of our seats, listening for whatever comes next. Remember, though, that while *I feel* can be a clue, we also have to listen for those non-feeling phrases, masquerading, and reactionary words that might be pointing back to an actual emotion.

The more fluent you become in the language of emotion, the better you'll get at recognizing emotional expressions and then connecting and relating in a deep and meaningful way.

In the words of Frasier Crane, "I'm listening."

## EMPATHY AND SYMPATHY

If you were drowning in a lake and a friend ran up to the shore and saw that you were struggling, would you want your friend to respond in a *sympathetic* way or an *empathic* way?

Need help deciding? Here's the difference:

- If your friend is *sympathetic*, he is going to jump in and, while drowning with you, look at you and talk about how horrible drowning is for you—and for him.

- If your friend is *empathic*, he is going to see how distraught you are, throw you a rope, and pull you in while worrying about you as he helps you out of the water.

Don't get me wrong: Sympathy has its place. It is important! In relationships, sympathy is like knowing the answers on an emotional test because you are feeling the same way. (Funeral, sad, me, my family—got it, we are all sad today!) This mutual emotional experience can create opportunities for connection; for example, going through a difficult time with others is helpful in the grieving process—as long as you are *moving through it together*.

Empathy is different from sympathy.

Our friends and even our clients regularly ask, "How do you listen to people talk about their problems all day long and not get burned out or overwhelmed with sadness?" Simple: We don't jump in the lake with them. We allow them to feel their sadness and fear. While we feel their sadness and fear, we keep ourselves separate by having our own emotional response. In contrast, sympathy would be having the same emotional response as the client without finding the way through the sadness and fear and instead drowning in it together.

Carl Rogers, a major influence on psychology and theory, defined empathy in his seminal work, *On Becoming a Person*. He defines empathic understanding as "sensing the feelings and personal meanings of people in each moment, perceiving these from 'inside,' as they seem to others, and then successfully communicating this understanding without losing the separateness of his own identity."[7] The keywords in this definition are *understanding, perceiving, communicating,* and *separateness*. Being empathic is about recognizing (understanding, perceiving, communicating) what someone is feeling without them having to say how they feel while at the same time keeping your feelings separate from the person with whom you are connecting.

Until you are fluent in the language of emotion, trying to be empathic can seem like an emotional guessing game. When you understand feelings, however, and know how to verbalize and pick up on emotional expressions, empathy becomes a powerful tool for emotional connection.

Now that we're on the same page with some of the basic terminology of this new language, let's talk about feelings.

# The Feeling Grid

Your intellect may be confused, but your
emotions never lie to you.
—*Roger Ebert*

**THE FEELING GRID HAS BECOME AN INTEGRAL PART OF OUR PRACTICE.** In this chapter, we'll explore its construction, purpose, and how to use it.

Before you continue to read through this chapter, spend some time on the next couple of pages looking at the Feeling Grid. Don't look for your feelings right now. (That's for later!) Instead, focus on the construction of the grid. What do you see in its architecture? How do the colors work? Compare the left side to the right side. After you have examined the grid, we will dive into discovering how this tool can help you.

**Download a printable copy of the Feeling Grid at FeelingGrid.com.**

| SAD | | |
|---|---|---|
| | Apathetic | Indifferent / Numb |
| | Hurt | Disappointed / Betrayed |
| | Lonely | Abandoned / Neglected |
| | Despair | Grief / Dejected |
| | Guilty | Remorseful / Miserable |
| | Shame | Worthless / Inferior |

| ANGRY | | |
|---|---|---|
| | Avoidant | Detached / Distant |
| | Defensive | Sarcastic / Exasperated |
| | Mad | Frustrated / Furious |
| | Selfish | Jealous / Envy |
| | Hateful | Resentment / Irritated |
| | Disgust | Appalled / Critical |

| FEAR | | |
|---|---|---|
| | Concerned | Confused / Embarrassed |
| | Rejected | Insignificant / Inadequate |
| | Scared | Discouraged / Exposed |
| | Helpless | Vulnerable / Useless |
| | Dread | Surprised / Apprehensive |
| | Anxious | Overwhelmed / Worried |

# The Feeling Grid

## JOYFUL

| | |
|---|---|
| Enthusiastic / Passionate | **Excited** |
| Fortunate / Appreciated | **Grateful** |
| Cherished / Noticed | **Whole** |
| Pleased / Elated | **Happy** |
| Liberated / Delighted | **Free** |
| Proud / Honored | **Hope** |

## EMPOWERED

| | |
|---|---|
| Present / Close | **Aware** |
| Connected / Caring | **Intimate** |
| Patient / Gentle | **Strong** |
| Validated / Confident | **Important** |
| Gracious / Faithful | **Respected** |
| Deserving / Admired | **Worthy** |

## PEACEFUL

| | |
|---|---|
| Nurtured / Reinforced | **Supported** |
| Significant / Acknowledged | **Accepted** |
| Encouraged / Protected | **Loved** |
| Safe / Trusted | **Secure** |
| Relieved / Certain | **Assured** |
| Relaxed / Satisfied | **Content** |

## TWO HALVES

The Feeling Grid is made up of two halves. It splits down the middle with what you might call "positive emotions" on the right and "negative emotions" on the left. While these terms seem to make sense, emotions are not positive or negative.

Emotions are emotions. They are present. Your experience or situation may be negative or positive, but the emotions you feel because of those events or circumstances simply exist. Your feelings are not good or bad; they are just how you feel.

If someone is sad about the loss of a loved one, the sadness they are experiencing is not bad. Losing someone we love or care about is simply sad. Is sad something we want to feel? Not usually, so there is probably a side you would prefer to be on. But both sides of the grid are necessary.

## SIX BASIC EMOTIONS

The Feeling Grid is composed of six basic emotions:
Sad
Anger
Fear
Peaceful
Empowered
Joy

Each of these six basic emotions serves as a header for its own smaller grid of related emotions. They are "basic" emotions, meaning they give you a place to start. Both the starting point and where you go from there as you move through the grid are important.

## Why These Six Basic Emotions?

The six basic emotions are rooted in the earliest ideas and research on emotions. Paul Ekman identified six emotions that were congruent across all cultures: happiness, sadness, fear, surprise, disgust, and anger.[8] We included each of these in the development of the Feeling Grid, although not all have their own headings. Surprise, for example, fits within the basic emotion of Fear, and disgust fits within the basic emotion of Anger.

During the past fifteen years of exploring the basic emotions presented in therapy, we have found that clients consistently use the labels of Sad, Anger, Fear, Peaceful, Empowered, and Joy. Sad, Anger, and Fear are easy to explain, which makes sense. Most people come to therapy because they feel sad, angry, or afraid. Rarely do we get a stream of new clients presenting with tons of happiness or wanting to discuss their abundant peace! The emotions on the left side of the Feeling Grid (Sad, Anger, Fear) are also consistent with Ekman's theory and proof that these three emotions relate across cultures.

The three basic emotions that are unique to the Feeling Grid and our theory of emotion are Joy, Empowered, and Peaceful. We chose Joy over happiness because of the word's range of feelings. There is a place for happiness within the Joy grid, of course. But Joy, rather than happiness, is the basic emotion. (We believe happiness is overrated, and you will learn why in Chapter 7.)

Peaceful evolved from the idea that clients did not always feel joy, happiness, or excitement but often felt a sense of peace for where they were in the moment. Or, in their words, they felt "good." We use the basic emotion of Peaceful to capture these *good* feelings. Peaceful is also the opposite of Fear. Agitation, trembling, or shaking (like tapping your foot when you are waiting to interview for a job) are often external demonstrations of fear, whereas physical movement isn't typically an indication of peaceful feelings.

Empowered found its spot on the right side of the Feeling Grid between Joy and Peace. We intentionally chose Empowered rather than powerful, a word on the Feeling Wheel that frequently failed to capture what clients described. The reason for this choice is twofold. First, *powerful* is not an emotion. Second, the term is difficult to use and promote in therapy, especially if we are working with clients on a marital issue or power differentiation. The label Empowered came from looking for an opposite of Anger. Anger aligns with power—pushing externally for what you want—whereas Empowered is something individually maintained from within. Chapter 9 focuses in-depth on Empowered.

## OPPOSITES

Each emotion in the Feeling Grid has an opposite emotion within the grid.

- The opposite of Sadness is Joy.
- The opposite of Fear is Peaceful.
- The opposite of Anger is Empowered.
- The mirroring of these words demonstrates the linear nature of the emotions on opposite sides of the Feeling Grid. The opposites exist beyond just the basic emotions. Each emotion on the grid has its opposite. Some of these might not be exactly what you expect, but we will explain our rationale.

## TIER-TWO EMOTIONS

The column to the right of the basic emotions of Sad, Anger, and Fear and the column to the left of the basic emotions of Joy, Empowered, and Peace include the Tier-Two emotions. Each of the six basic emotions has six emotions that are more specific in Tier Two. For example, Sad could be described as Apathetic, Hurt, Lonely, Despair, Guilty, or Shame. Take a look at the Feeling Grid and look through the other Tier-Two emotions for Anger, Fear, Joy, Empowered, and Peace. Do you relate to some of these feelings right now? Can you tell the difference between feeling hurt (Sad) or having concern (Fear)?

Tier-Two emotions are related to the basic emotions but have subtle differences. These secondary emotions expand the basic emotion and offer more insight into how you feel or how the person with whom you are connecting feels. Four clients in a row might talk about sadness in session, and each one can feel sad for a different reason. One may be dealing with feeling guilty, for example, while another feels apathetic. Both are forms of sadness, but these Tier-Two emotions allow us to gain deeper understanding of the basic emotion.

With other clients, the Tier-Two emotions direct us toward the basic emotion. Clients often say things like, "I'm just a little lonely. That's all." When we look at the Feeling Grid together, they can see that loneliness is a form of sadness. Whether we are connecting from the Tier-Two emotion to the basic emotion or from the basic emotion to the Tier-Two emotion, the clarity gained is helpful in developing emotional awareness, connection, and working through issues.

## Internally Experienced

Tier-Two emotions tend to relate to us in the first person, and they present as internal experiences. Because you experience them internally, your Tier-Two emotions are not always obvious to others. The Tier-Two emotion of rejection, for example, falls within the basic emotion of Fear. Rejection is an internal experience, meaning you can feel rejected without anyone knowing how you feel.

For every internally experienced Tier-Two emotion, there are two more expressive emotions that others may recognize (or potentially misinterpret) by your words, tone of voice, posture, or behavior. This brings us to Tier-Three emotions.

## TIER-THREE EMOTIONS

The two center columns on the Feeling Grid are the Tier-Three emotions. The Tier-Three columns include two new emotion expressions for each Tier-Two emotion.

**Example**: When someone is angry and feels defensive, they express their anger using sarcasm.

*Anger* (basic emotion) → *Defensive* (Tier Two, an internal feeling)

→ *Sarcastic* (Tier Three, an external expression of emotion)

The goal of moving from the basic emotion through Tier-Two feelings and connecting with a Tier-Three emotion is to become more knowledgeable about how you feel. When you can identify how you feel and are clearly able to verbalize those feelings, you are better equipped to connect emotionally with others.

Knowing your basic emotion is a great place to start. It gives you insight into yourself and those with whom you are connecting. There is a need, however, to move toward specificity. Without identifying precise feelings, you are not giving an accurate insight into your feelings or what is important to you.

One couple, we'll call them Joe and Sherry, came to therapy for more than a year. We met with them separately and as a couple. The long-term struggles of their forty-plus years of marriage came to a head when Sherry discovered Joe had texted inappropriate pictures to a neighbor. Sherry often began sessions by stating her basic emotion, "I feel sad." Identifying that feeling was important, but it did not offer a full description of her feelings. Tier-Two emotions narrowed down the region of her emotion. "I feel hurt," she would say. This created a path for greater connection to the feelings Sherry had experienced in the relationship. She was not feeling apathy or guilt; she felt hurt.

Finally, the Tier-Three emotion gave a precise location for her emotionally: "I feel betrayed." Absolutely! With that, she provided deeper knowledge of her feelings. She did not feel inferior or indifferent, nor was she grieving. Understanding that she felt betrayed gave Joe the insight he needed to comfort Sherry's true emotion.

## Extreme vs. Unique

Tier-Three emotions serve to help us identify the degree of feeling (mild to extreme) or specificity (the unique emotion) of Tier-Two emotions.

The Tier-Three emotions of Anxious are Worried and Overwhelmed. These emotions describe the degree to which someone feels anxious with Worried being less anxious than Overwhelmed. Susan and I both felt anxious as we handed the car keys to our daughter for the first time. We experienced that emotion to different degrees. Susan was worried about our daughter driving for the first time. I felt overwhelmed knowing our daughter was heading out onto the highway. Both of us felt anxious, but how we experienced that emotion was different.

The degree of difference in Tier-Three emotions can be subtle difference, so let's use Mad for the next example. Tier-Three emotions for Mad are Frustrated and Furious. Furious is more mad than Frustrated. When our daughter got a speeding ticket, Susan sighed and let her know she felt frustrated (because Susan is not new to speeding tickets). Our daughter might have felt concerned about telling her mom about the ticket, but she dreaded telling me because she knew I would be furious.

Tier-Three emotions are also used to help categorize and describe how these unique emotions directly relate to the Tier-Two emotion. Sometimes, it is not about understanding the degree of the emotion but identifying the specific emotion you feel. In the Sad grid, a Tier-Two emotion is Despair. The Tier-Three emotions related to Despair are Grief and Dejected. While there are degrees of Grief and degrees of Dejected, these two emotions are unique. It is important to know which feeling is present, Grief or Dejected. One of these provides an understanding that there is loss. The other is simply a deeper level of sadness.

### Externally Expressed

Tier-Three emotions are expressed in an external way, either verbally or behaviorally—or both. Let's use Exasperated, which Susan has expressed as we are writing this section of the book. She shows this in her facial expression and crossed arms, as well as mentioning how particularly exasperating my edits have been. She must be feeling defensive about my editing suggestions. Exasperated (Tier-Three emotion) is expressed externally as a reflection of her internally experienced emotion of Defensive (Tier-Two emotion).

## FINDING YOUR EMOTIONS

Now that you are familiar with the layout and flow of the Feeling Grid, it's time to learn how to use it to find your emotion. The Feeling Grid can and should be used bidirectionally. You can start with a basic emotion and work your way through each tier to identify the specific emotion that gives you more understanding of where you are in the moment. Or you can start with a Tier-Two or a Tier-Three emotion, working backward from the specific emotion in Tier Three to gain the knowledge of what is happening internally in the Tier-Two and basic emotion.

If the only emotion you can use to describe your current experience is Sad—that is a great start. But don't stop there. The clearer you are about how you feel, the greater the ability you have to connect with someone by sharing that information.

Let's take a more in-depth look at how to work with the Feeling Grid bidirectionally.

### Basic to Specific

When we ask clients, "What are you feeling?" and hear crickets paired with a blank or confused look, we hand them the Feeling Grid and say, "Let's start with the basic emotions." Clients can then choose the basic emotion they are feeling, or they can begin by ruling out the emotions they are not feeling.

Sometimes, it comes down to the battle of two emotions, say sad and angry. But when we look at the Tier-Two emotions for each of these basic emotions, clients can better clarify how they feel. From there, they can move to the next tier to create more specificity.

The accuracy of your feelings can deepen your connection with what you are feeling. If you aren't sure what you're feeling, starting with the basic emotion can be helpful.

## Specific to Basic

If you have an understanding of emotions, you might start with a more specific emotion in Tier Three (or Tier Two). Describing your emotion with a more specific emotion does not mean you have a full insight into your emotion and how it is affecting you. Even if you start in a more specific tier, moving toward the basic emotion creates a greater clarity of what you are feeling.

One common statement we hear is, "I'm not mad; I am just frustrated." Tracing frustrated from Tier Three back to the basic emotion, we see that frustrated *is* mad. If you feel frustrated, you are acting out of anger. Specific is informative, but remember to go back to the basics for clarity of emotion.

## Using Opposites

"No respect, I get no respect!" Poor Rodney Dangerfield. The comedian was a man before his time with emotion, but he was on to something with his famous catchphrase. He identified what he was experiencing, "no respect," and figured out what he needed: respect.

When clients do not know or cannot express how they feel, we ask, "How do you want to feel?" Often, they come back with phrases like, "I just want to feel safe," or "I wish I could feel supported," or, like Dangerfield, "Can I just have some respect?"

Using opposites on the Feeling Grid will give you a place to start as you work to understand your emotions. Try it: Go to the Feeling Grid and find the emotion that you want to feel. Then, trace that feeling to the opposite side of the grid. The words you find there will help you identify what emotion you are currently experiencing.

## HOW DOES COLOR RELATE?

The first part of this chapter has been used to teach you how to move from left and right to gain an understanding of how linear our emotions are when relating to others (and self). Now, we are going to zoom out and allow the colors within the Feeling Grid to help us relate in a different way. The spectrum of colors in the Feeling Grid represents the fluidity of emotion, while the perceptions of the colors of the grid help us understand the constant presence of emotion, even as our feelings change from moment to moment.

### Color Spectrum

Emotion does not stop and start. There are no pauses between changes of emotion. Emotion is a fluid experience. What is important to know is that emotions overlap both horizontally and vertically on the Feeling Grid.

Let's look at Anxious as an example of the fluid experience of emotion. Anxious is a Tier-Two emotion found at the bottom of the left side of the grid within the basic emotion of Fear. Anxious could be described as *not knowing what is about to happen or how you are going to feel in the future.* Wouldn't you agree that this could easily become a dreadful experience or, perhaps, an exciting one? Dread is directly above Anxious, while Excitement is directly below Anxious. Dread is Fear, while Excitement is Joy. Both stem from Anxious. The purpose of the color spectrum in the Feeling Grid is to help you remember that emotion is *a continuous sequence of order or range* and flows throughout the entire Feeling Grid.

The problem is we don't learn where some emotions begin and others end. Spending time with the Feeling Grid dispels the myth that emotions are mutually exclusive; emotions are continuous and overlapping. When you identify your emotion, it is also important to notice whether there is any overlap with any other emotions.

We can have multiple feelings, but this overlap can help "triangulate" your emotional location. The color spectrum of the Feeling Grid illustrates this natural overlap of the wide range and sequence of emotions that exist.

## Perceptions

Red is a basic color that's easy to identify. This primary color, however, has many shades and tints, all with different names. One person's brick red is another person's barn red—and both reds take on different tones based on the lighting. Similarly, while emotions are fluid, each person's perception of an emotion can be rigid.

Our feelings are perceptions that define and describe our individual experiences. Even if we all have an understanding of an emotion like sadness, our perceptions of that emotion can vary. What is important, then, when considering others' emotions is to listen for what others feel (how *they* perceive the emotion). You might not feel sad in the moment, for example, but you know what sadness is. If someone tells you they are sad, you understand what it means to feel sad, and you can acknowledge that their sadness exists even if you are not sad at the moment.

---

*Our feelings are perceptions that define and describe our **individual** experiences.*

---

Here's another example: I will never be able to convince Susan that a cockroach, dead or alive, is not a scary thing. I find the presence of a cockroach unwelcome, but I am not frightened by the insect. I could explain the lack of danger posed by a cockroach or the irrationality of her beliefs, but none of that is going to keep her from shuddering at the sight of an upside-down cockroach in the garage. To connect with her emotionally when she's freaked out by a cockroach, it is not important for me to understand why she is afraid. Nor do I have to be afraid of the bug myself. What's important is that I understand she is afraid. I know fear, and I can comfort her fear. To question or challenge her fear would not help us connect; in fact, it might create more emotions and problems in our relationship.

The spectrum of emotion gives people with different perceptions the ability to connect and relate. Simply stated, if I had to relate to someone and there were only six emotions in the world, I would have a one-in-six chance. But when each basic emotion has eighteen versions of the basic emotion, I have eighteen chances to connect correctly.

## A TOOL FOR CLARITY AND CONNECTION

The Feeling Grid is not an exhaustive list of emotions. There may be words you want to add, and there may be some words on the Feeling Grid that are not part of your regular vocabulary. You might even need to look up the definitions of a few of the emotions. (To help you, we provide some definitions at the end of each chapter.)

Our clients' input through the past two decades has been essential to the development of the Feeling Grid. After all, the goal is to become more specific or accurate in expressing our emotions. We do that by listening for what resonates and what's missing. I mentioned previously that I am vigilant about listening for feeling words. I paid attention when clients perused the Feeling Grid and asked why they couldn't find "annoyed" or "numb" or "shocked." Through the years, we've added words as necessary to provide needed clarity. Other times, we could point to suitable synonyms. One of the last words added to the Feeling Grid was Dread. Susan wasn't convinced at first that people would resonate with *dread*, but the next week, three of her clients and one of mine pointed to the word to describe their feelings.

The more our clients use this tool, the better they are able to describe emotions for themselves. At the same time, their experiences have expanded the understanding Susan and I have of how emotions work for individuals and in relationships. Together, we and our clients have noticed the power of this tool as both emotional awareness and emotional connection have grown. We've also noticed that the more we look for emotions, the more (and more clearly) we see and hear them in action—at home, at work, at the store, and even in the media.

Our goal with this book is to equip you with the language of emotion and empower you to identify where you are so you can better understand yourself *and* connect with other people. Our hope is that thus far, you have learned . . .

- Emotions exist. They are not good or bad but only present.
- Emotions are the path to human connection.
- Being *emotional* is having emotional awareness. It's different from being reactive.
- Understanding your emotions is critical to your self-esteem, relationships, and overall mental well-being.
- Emotional awareness empowers you to better understand yourself and others.
- The more you understand about yourself and the people in your life, the greater chance you have of experiencing better relationships.
- You create that understanding and connection by listening intently for emotional expressions.
- The Feeling Grid is a powerful tool that you can use anytime to understand and better communicate how you are feeling.

The Feeling Grid has become an essential tool in our practice. It connects with multiple theories of psychology, including emotion-focused therapy, interpersonal process, humanistic (person-centered), psychodynamics, and more. Whether you are a mental health professional using this tool with your clients or are an individual who is seeking to improve your emotional awareness, we trust that you will find the Feeling Grid to be a useful resource. Bookmark or dog-ear the Feeling Grid so you can refer to it easily as you continue learning the language of emotion.

In the next six chapters, we are going to expand the discussion of the Feeling Grid through the basic emotions, starting with the one that is most overused and abused: Anger.

# Anger

> Years of love have been forgot in the hatred of a minute.
> —*Edgar Allan Poe*

**EVERY CLIENT WHO WALKS INTO OUR PRACTICE STRUGGLES WITH ANGER.** Chances are good that if you are struggling emotionally or relationally, it's because you are struggling with anger. That sounds like a bold statement, and you may have already crossed your arms and said, "Not me." If that's the case, you aren't alone. A lot of our clients disagree that anger could be the problem—at first. So stay with us.

Anger is ground zero. It's where we most often begin when using the Feeling Grid. Understanding the theory of anger will change how you relate to everyone in your life—even the telemarketer who calls four times a day.

## Pop Quiz: What kind of angry are you?

Anger presents itself in three different ways. Read the anger statements and the phrases below. Make note of which one sounds like something you might think or say.

1) **Anger is what helps you through hard times, so anger is a good thing.**

   Of course I get angry. How else would I survive?
   Anger keeps me from getting walked all over.
   The only way my husband knows he is wrong is if I get angry at him.

2) **Anger exists in you, and you want it to go away because you know it hurts you and others.**

   My anger is out of control.
   All I do is end up hurting the people I love.
   Anger always gets me into trouble.

3) **You are not one who uses anger. You don't believe that you share or express anger, ever.**

   I don't get angry.
   I'm not an angry person.
   I never get mad and yell at anyone.

Which of the phrases do you relate to most? Can you see how people use anger in completely different ways? That's what makes anger so fascinating! Some people accept and embrace the use of anger, while others don't even recognize their anger exists. Still others seek therapy because they want to make their anger go away.

## Is anger useful?

Rick[*] had never been in a significant romantic relationship. It wasn't all that surprising that, even in his mid-sixties, Rick struggled to connect with people in meaningful ways. His parents' marriage had provided a poor example of what relationships looked like through their angry outbursts and avoidance of any expression of sadness when, for example, someone died

---

[*] All names and details have been changed to honor our clients' confidentiality.

or when he was hurt. As a child, his peers told him he was strange and not worth being around. Early on, anger became his go-to emotion.

Rick's dad told him to use his anger to do well in sports because that's where he would gain respect from others. Rick spent his high school years unleashing his anger on his opponents on the field. When Rick made a mistake on the field, he used that to fuel his anger even more to help the team win. "My anger helped us win games," he confessed. But it did not help him win with others. His relationships with his teammates did not improve.

If Rick had not focused so intently on using his anger on the field, might he have found that his self-confidence and connection with teammates were more empowering and more satisfying? We can't say for sure. What we do know, however, is that Rick came to counseling because he felt alone and incapable of forming healthy relationships.

Anger may have led to a win for the game, but it only created more problems when it came to relationships. Rick's anger was rooted in his fear and sadness that developed over years of not relating to his parents, friends at school, or coworkers when he was an adult. Anger does not leave room to grow and emotionally connect.

Rick isn't alone. It's common to hear clients say things like, "Anger helps you power through." Power is simply another word for anger. Powering through is how people end up disconnecting. Reacting with anger only creates more anger, which is why, more than any other emotion, anger leads to lost jobs, hurt spouses, and estranged families. So let's consider an alternative to making anger the main source of action or communication when threatened.

## **ANGER EXISTS FROM THE BEGINNING**

There are two kinds of newborns: babies and angry babies. Yes, we love babies. Newborns are adorable! They are also angry. Sure, sometimes babies give Dad a grin when they pass gas or mimic Mom's smile with one of their own. Have you noticed how much they cry, though? A lot.

When infants are hungry, want to be picked up or put to sleep, require a diaper change, or have any other basic need, they yell at you. It's not a cry of sadness; it's a cry of demand—for help. Anger is a tool babies use instinctively, not out of meanness or hatred but for *protection*.

Infants have no ability to protect themselves. A kitten can crawl to their mother to nurse. A foal can walk within an hour after being born and can run within two hours. Not us. Newborn humans are completely dependent upon others for protection. So we cry out, demanding that protection.

Eventually, we outgrow the need to get angry and cry for food. Babies learn to root for their mother's nipple, and toddlers learn to say, "I'm hungry." Teens learn how to use DoorDash.

It would stand to reason that as physical growth alleviates our need to get angry and cry out for help, our instinctive response should evolve, but we all still use anger for protection. Unfortunately, anger doesn't go away. We don't need it anymore because we can express what we need. So why does anger remain? What are we protecting ourselves from?

We are protecting ourselves from the other uncomfortable emotions—the ones we are taught *not* to feel: sadness and fear.

The basic emotions of Sadness and Fear fuel the existence of all expressions of anger. They are also the emotions people typically want to avoid. Why? In part because sadness and fear aren't fun to experience. They don't feel good. In twenty years of practice, never has a client

---

*The basic emotions of Sadness and Fear fuel the existence of all expressions of anger.*

## Disclaimer for Anger in Traumatic Events

When we share our theory of anger being a reaction that does not work in the moment, we typically get pushback. This pushback and further discussion with clients and group participants helped us further develop our theory of anger.

We believe there is one scenario in which anger is useful and, at times, even necessary, and that is within a traumatic event. When someone describes their childhood, for example, as one where they felt they had to use physical displays of anger to survive, we don't dispute that choice. **Surviving any type of trauma is the solution to trauma, and if anger is what was used, we accept and applaud this interaction.** In sessions with these people, we explore how anger was necessary in the traumatic scenario *and* how it is not a tool that works outside of that event or environment. Nor is it an emotion that can help them heal from the trauma.

Julia Cameron, in her book *The Artist's Way*, appeals to how we think about anger in moments of personal protection: "Anger is meant to be acted upon. It is not meant to be acted out. Anger points the direction. We are meant to use anger as fuel to take the actions we need to move where our anger points. With a little thought, we can usually translate the message that our anger is sending us."[9]

come in for therapy because they want to continue to feel sad or fearful. Additionally, society perpetuates the myth that admitting to or showing either of these emotions is a weakness.

Anger protects us from *feeling* sad or fearful. Note that sadness and fear are still present. We are simply covering up those emotions and distracting ourselves with anger.

Useful, harmful, instinctual, or protective—however you decide to label or dress up anger—it exists, and it isn't leaving. Learning how to maintain it is the key and the purpose of this book. While anger does not work, it does exist. Allowing it to grow and using it as your emotional shield can be destructive and isolating. Allowing sadness and fear into your relationships, however, can create a stronger connection with others and yourself.

Learning what your anger looks like and understanding what you're trying *not* to feel is the first step to better emotional connection.

## What does your anger look like?

Susan here. Let's take that first step together.

Your personality began developing as soon as you could walk and interact with others. The same is true for the type of anger you exhibit. The interactions you experienced during your formative years, particularly the way you saw anger expressed, taught you how to express anger. I remember scolding our children once and immediately thinking, *I sound just like my mother*. Of course I did. We all learn from what we experience.

Each of us develops an *anger imprint*. It's the way we react when we feel angry—regardless of whether that anger stems from sadness or fear. To understand what your anger imprint is, take a look at the Feeling Grid. First, consider the Tier-Two emotions beside *Angry*. When you feel angry, how do you react most often?

- **Avoidant**—Do you shut down, avoiding the person or circumstance?
- **Defensive**—Do you become defensive, putting verbal, mental, or even physical barriers around yourself?
- **Mad**—Do you lash out with a rant or find yourself in a spiral of anger?
- **Selfish**—Are you focusing only on what you want?
- **Hateful**—Do you count up all the wrongs a person has committed and hold a grudge?
- **Disgust**—Do you think, *I can't even look at or talk to them*?

Once you've identified the Tier-Two word that best applies to the way you experience anger (at least most of the time), take a look at the corresponding Tier-Three words. Which best describes the way you behave when you feel angry?

Your anger imprint is the way you habitually deal with anger. When you pause to look at the Feeling Grid, you can probably find the words that best describe how you use anger. If you're in a long-term relationship, like Bryan and I after twenty years of marriage, you can probably identify the anger imprint of the person or people closest to you. Heck, I've got my two kids' anger imprints down, as well as my mom's—you guessed it—because we are all similar and passing it down generationally.

Bryan and I both tend to be avoidant but for different reasons. When I am angry, I stop talking and start building my case—my reasons to be angry—mentally. I use Avoidance while tapping into Hateful and Disgust. I find what I resent and become critical. I'll silently list all that the other person did wrong while detaching from the person or circumstance as much as possible. As much as I feel like I might explode, I also don't want to hurt people with my words. I know my anger imprint is kicking in when I stop talking and feel myself shutting down (avoidance). It is my responsibility to work on not staying angry or getting angrier.

Interestingly, Bryan's anger imprint is also avoidant, although until he started exploring emotion-based therapy, he thought he never got angry. He is a *quiet* angry person; he doesn't yell. He shuts down. Our differences show up in Tier Three. Bryan stays in avoidance, and he detaches and creates distance until he feels welcomed back in.

Our behavior looks similar, but his anger imprint of avoidance is based in trying to distance and protect himself, whereas mine comes from a desire to prove it wasn't me who is to blame for anyone's pain or suffering.

When you understand your anger imprint, you can be more aware of the possibility of hurting someone. More importantly, you become more aware of the fact you are either sad or fearful in the moment. You may decide that allowing yourself to acknowledge that you feel confused or embarrassed (fear) or hurt and betrayed (sad) is better than allowing your anger to continue to build.

## ANGER IS A REACTION

Most people think of anger like the fiery red, mustache-wearing hothead in the *Inside Out* movies. (If you haven't seen it, you should.) The Disney Pixar adaptation of Anger yells. He kicks and screams. He blows his top and stomps loudly. Our clients often balk at the idea of anger being part of their emotional repertoire because they *don't* scream, stomp, or slam doors. But that fireball's display is not the only way anger presents itself. For a lot of people, anger is a far cry from shouting. Sometimes anger presents as seething, sulking, or quietly sounding off under one's breath, which can make it difficult for some people to own up to the idea that they are angry.

I was appointed by the court to work with Sarah and John while they were going through a divorce. The couple was incapable of mediation or being in the presence of each other. Due to the amount of anger present on both sides, the judge mandated counseling for each family member on an individual basis from the same counselor, in the hopes of finding a common denominator within the couples' communication. How was I, simply a licensed professional counselor, supposed to dissolve this much anger in a couple that not even the courts and all the attorneys could unravel. As I read through their documents, the hostility was palpable. Everybody's goal was to get through the divorce without any further delay, emotions aside. My goal: Bring emotions front and center. It was my only tool.

When I met with Sarah, she described John's anger as volatile, the spitting image of Anger on *Inside Out*, but not cartoonish or humorous in any way. His loud rants had become an almost daily occurrence. At least, that's what it seemed like to Sarah. Sarah presented very calm and quiet and said she was never angry. I knew right then that she didn't know what her anger looked like.

Sarah talked mostly about her sadness at the marriage dissolving. Not knowing how to deal with their crumbling relationship, Sarah shut down emotionally. In the two years leading up to the divorce, she stayed in her room whenever he was home (avoidant).

And there it was: Sarah reacted with detachment and distance.

"So when your husband came home, you avoided talking to him?" I asked.

"Yes, that seemed to be the best way to protect myself," she replied.

"So you reacted to his anger . . . with anger."

She shook her head. "No, I wasn't angry. I was protecting myself by distancing myself from him."

Like so many people, Sarah didn't realize protecting herself by shutting down was a form of anger. Her anger imprint was to shut down—to avoid and distance herself from her husband. Sarah's anger looked very different from her husband's, but it was still a reaction that created more distance between her and her husband. As we progressed in therapy, Sarah realized her reaction to John's anger, shutting down, had started early in their marriage.

As Sarah and John came to counseling separately, I noticed their anger easing. They each realized they were both experiencing feelings of fear and sadness driving their anger, and they were able to see one another more clearly. In the end, the couple reunited because they were able to connect emotionally.

Anger is a reaction that covers true emotion. If you think of anger as a reaction, it becomes something you don't need to express.

> *Anger is a reaction that covers true emotion.*

## The Reaction Box

One of my goals with clients is to learn how their specific type of anger presents itself in the moment. When I ask them how they would describe themselves when they get angry, just like Sarah, most clients initially deny that they are angry or rarely, if ever, feel angry. They can, however, look at the words under Anger and immediately find a feeling word that describes their way of dealing with anger—even if they're "not an angry person."

I dubbed the orange area on the left side of the Feeling Grid the Anger Box. We spent so much time in sessions pointing to this section of the Feeling Grid that it seemed more efficient to give it a name. Calling it the Anger Box also softened the blow when calling out a client for being angry. Saying, "*Hmm*, I think you are hanging out in the Anger Box," sounds a lot better than, "You look angry!"

Over time, though, I also noticed how frequently clients used the term *reaction* when describing their anger: "I did not want to react that way" or "I wish I hadn't reacted that way." That description popped up so often that I added the label *Reaction Box* to the list of ways to describe anger with clients.

Just like pointing clients to the Anger Box or the Reaction Box, the focus is not as heavily on what the client is doing wrong or how angry they look, but more on learning about their reactions and how to shift out of reacting and into feeling. Besides, *reaction* has a much better reputation than anger, and it's easier for people to put into context:

- Wincing when you stub your toe is a reaction.
- Hanging up the phone on someone is a reaction.
- Shouting at your spouse is a reaction.
- Shutting down when you remember you can't call your mom because she passed away is a reaction.
- Walking out on your marriage is a reaction.
- Crying when someone confronts you is a reaction.

Webster's Dictionary defines *reaction* as "to act in opposition to a force or influence—usually used with the word against." Do you notice the subtlety of the use of power in this definition? *Opposition, against, force.* A reaction pushes away. It is an act that creates a disconnect between you and the person with whom you are trying to connect.

A few pages back, we posed the question: *Is anger useful?* If you consider that anger is a reaction that pushes others away, it is easy to see how useless and unproductive anger can be for connecting with or relating to others. Hmm, could we also call the orange box on the left the *Power Box*?

## POWER VS. PROTECTION

Because we offer marriage counseling, we have front-row seats to watch how people use anger in relationships. In fact, it was through counseling couples that we identified the two categories of reactions that anger elicits: *power* and *protection*.

## Power Reaction

Power is an external reaction that is used to maintain control within the relationship. Sometimes, a power reaction looks or sounds hostile, like an attack. It may not be a physical attack (although that would be a power reaction) but a verbal one that the person uses to try to prove their point or get their way. Those who use anger as a power reaction may list everything the other person has done wrong or let others know how sacrificial they are being in the moment. If an argument ensues, people with this kind of anger reaction will be determined to prove their point, be in the right, and win.

## Protection Reaction

Protection is typically an internal reaction that, as the word implies, serves to protect someone from the relationship. These reactions include behaviors such as shutting down, backing off, or choosing to ignore what is happening. Those who rely on a protection reaction might acquiesce or agree (even when they don't). If someone tries to engage them in an argument, they might walk away. If they predict an argument could be on the horizon, they might make themselves scarce or avoid certain topics in hopes of dodging the conflict completely.

## How do you react?

When couples argue, each person has a goal either to protect themselves or to prove a point (aka win), which is why we often ask couples how they argue. Their answers can spotlight their type of reaction. But you don't have to be married or dating to identify your reaction type. You don't even have to have an argument.

Recall your anger imprint—the way you habitually react when you feel angry. Think about the way you argue, then take a few minutes to answer the following questions.

- Do you intentionally avoid specific topics or people?
- Do you ignore problems in your relationships?
- Do you shut down?
- Do you walk away from an argument?
- Do you hang up on people?
- Do you wear headphones to avoid or ignore someone?
- Do you focus on protecting yourself in the relationship?

If you answered yes to the questions above, you are using a protection reaction.

- Do you become critical of others?
- Do you bring out what happened last week to prove you are not wrong or that you have a right to be mad?
- Do you feel disgusted by others' words or behaviors?
- Do you stomp your feet or slam doors?
- Do you use harsh words?
- Do you use sarcasm to make your point?
- Do you work hard to prove your *truth*?
- Do you try to maintain power within the relationship?

If you answered yes to the questions above, you are using a power reaction. But here's a twist: Even if you are reacting powerfully, you are doing so because you are trying to protect something.

Understanding your anger imprint and reaction type is important for two reasons. First, it helps you recognize when you are angry and that you do actually get angry. Second, when you are emotionally aware enough to notice your anger reaction, you can take the next steps to figure out where the reaction is coming from (other emotions we will learn in Chapters 5 through 9).

It's worth noting that *neither* reaction type is better than the other. Both power and protection reactions are red flags that you are hanging out in the orange box on the left side of the grid, whether you call it the Anger Box, Reaction Box, Protection Box, or Power Box.

## ANGER DOESN'T WORK

Sharing emotions is meant to build relationships, but anger does the opposite. Using emotion to connect requires both awareness of your true feelings and a willingness to share those feelings.

Anger fails at both.

The illusion anger offers is that it empowers you with control over yourself (by protecting you) or control of others or your circumstances (giving you the power in the relationship). In reality, anger *dis*empowers you. It's a reaction (one that is rarely well thought out) that prevents you from connecting with others or yourself. It isolates you from others emotionally and, sometimes, physically. Beyond that, when you use anger, you are giving away any power or control over yourself. Deciding to share your true emotions, such as fear or sadness, is what creates the ability to feel empowered. The more time you spend understanding your anger imprint and what you are trying to achieve when using it, the more

> *When you use anger, you are giving away any power or control over yourself.*

evident it will become that anger eliminates any feeling of control or power. Feeling out of control and without power makes it difficult to connect. If you want to connect with others, you must first concede your anger and then identify the underlying emotions responsible for it.

Remember, sadness and fear are the two basic emotions that fuel the existence of all expressions of anger. If you look again at the Feeling Grid, you'll see that when people feel sad, they are looking for joy. How does anger lead to joy? It doesn't! When people are afraid, they are seeking peace. How does anger lead to peace? It doesn't!

Think about the last time you got angry. Was this anger helping you feel either joy or peace? Probably not.

Whatever the significance or level of your relationship, be it with a friend, boss, neighbor, your spouse, or child, anger will never help you find joy or peace and the ultimate feeling of being empowered. Anger only creates more anger. You can think of it this way: Anger is out of control (seen externally); empowered is in control (felt internally).

## When Anger Doesn't Work

I (Susan) had a client who professed to hating humans. She grew up an only child with nobody ever talking to her. She recalled her parents arguing or ignoring each other but never any meaningful conversations or attention involving her. To her, it made sense to "hate humans." She found a job that did not involve too much human interaction and, after thirty years, recently retired. She had also been caring for her mom, the last person in her family still alive, and her mom passed away, which prompted her to find counseling. She was all alone, an orphan, she said, which created even more anger.

You might think my client's anger is the focus; it's not. My anger is the focus of this story. I kept getting mad at how she described humans, called them names, and concluded that all humans were horrible. But I was a human, and I thought I was pretty nice.

Session one, I let her talk and reflected as a good counselor does.

Session two, the lawn guy was an idiot, her phone carrier rep was stupid, and she didn't like how her neighbor parked his car.

Session three, I began planning my therapeutic escape. I had not reacted to her at all. My battle as to why I couldn't let her continue ranting in therapy happened in my head. Listening, after all, was my job. I thought about referring her to another counselor on our team who would have more patience than me.

Session four, she discussed how angry she was about how her mom died. I saw an opening. Losing someone is definitively connected to sadness. She refused to let go of her anger, but my anger subsided a bit because I knew sadness had to be close by. Instead of referring her to another counselor or shutting down my empathy because I felt beat up as a fellow human for the last three sessions—I started sharing about my brother's death. As I shared how I lost my brother, I expected her to interrupt, but she leaned in and just listened. I understood what it felt like to have no control over saving that one very important person. Her face softened, and she sat for a few seconds and said, "Wow, I am so sorry you lost your brother that way." I smiled, and there was the connection.

When it was just her anger and my anger in the room, there was no connection. I needed that door of connecting to open just a little bit. Did her anger disappear? No, but that little opening of non-anger created a path to her reactions to other humans decreasing over time and the ability to do some therapeutic work for future relationships to exist in her life.

## THE PURPOSE OF ANGER

Here's a quick recap of what we've covered so far regarding anger:
- In infancy, humans use anger for protection.
- Humans continue to use anger for protection or to gain power, which is a form of self-protection.
- Anger does not work as a means of building emotional connection or getting your needs met.
- Anger is a reaction.

# An Engaged, Supportive Pillar

Reacting in anger is natural for humans. It's an instinctive cry for protection. Reacting in anger, however, can become habitual, and staying angry is a learned behavior.

If reacting out of anger is not the way to communicate, then what are you supposed to do? The answer to that is to *respond*. Let's compare the definition of *react* (to act in opposition to a force or influence) to that of *respond*:

## Respond
(verb)

*1: to say something in return: make an answer.*

*2: to show a favorable reaction.*

It's intentional. A *favorable* reaction. One that doesn't push people away. But there's more to responding than that. When I looked up *respond* in the dictionary, I fell in love with the noun's definition. It is a perfect depiction of what we can create when we choose not to react in anger:

## Respond
(noun)

*an engaged pillar supporting an arch or closing a colonnade or arcade.*

Isn't that beautiful?
Be the engaged, supportive pillar. Stop reacting. Learn how to respond.

- Reacting in anger creates more anger.
- Each person has an anger imprint.
- All reactions of anger are precipitated by true emotions of fear and sadness.
- Anger is not going away.

I told you anger was fascinating! Fascinating in the *unraveling of something unknown in the world that has an illimitable effect on all relationships*. Anger can also be devastating to our entire well-being. Anger simply doesn't work. So are we suggesting that you should never get angry? Is that even possible? Does anger have a purpose?

Anthropologist Jean Briggs spent seventeen months in the frozen tundra of the Northwest Territories of Canada with an Inuit tribe called the Utkuhikhalingmiut (good luck with that pronunciation) considering that question. In most cultures, anger is overused, even celebrated. In the Utkuhikhalingmiut culture, anger is never outwardly expressed. The tribe teaches its children that anger is never acceptable because it can injure people.

In *Never in Anger*, her book chronicling her experience with the Utkuhikhalingmiut, Briggs explained that she learned this lesson the hard way early in her time with the group. Some white (non-Inuit) fishermen had come into the area and had broken boats belonging to the Utkuhikhalingmiut. Angry on behalf of the Inuit, she says, "I lost my temper (very mildly as we ourselves would view it) . . . This incident brought to a head a long-standing uneasiness on the part of the Eskimos [Inuit] concerning my un-Eskimo volatility, and as a result of my unseemly and frightening wrath at the fishermen I was ostracized, very subtly, for about three months."[10] The silent treatment she received prompted her to study the way the people expressed emotion, and as the title of the book reveals, anger, even what we might consider "righteous anger," was never an acceptable reaction.

The Utkuhikhalingmiuts do not permit outward displays of anger, but I would argue that anger probably still exists in that culture. Even the example of Briggs being ostracized for her anger points to the anger reaction of shutting down. That's simply an internal expression rather than an external one, quiet but ineffective. It took more than three months to resolve the misunderstanding!

In her study of the Utkuhikhalingmiut, Briggs noticed a lack of expression of other emotions as well—and we don't want that!

Going back to the central theme of this book, we—individuals, couples, families, communities, and society at large—*need* emotional connection. This brings us to the purpose of anger, which is to recognize underlying feelings. Anger waves the red flag to alert you that you are feeling sad or fearful. The red flag is a warning that you that if you do not take caution, your anger will overtake you.

> *Without anger, you might not even know that what you're feeling is sadness or fear.*

Anger allows you to notice that you are feeling an emotion—one that may be difficult to talk about. In fact, without anger, you might not even know that what you're feeling is sadness or fear.

You will get better at recognizing sadness and fear as you move through this book, but the best place to start is to identify your anger.

When do you use your anger?

Toward whom is your anger directed?

Do you only show anger at home?

Are you angry at yourself more than anyone else?

Why do you argue?

Pay attention to your anger. Study it, define it, take a cross section of its existence, and label every layer. Spend time with your anger! Like anything else you conquer in life, you have to know it well enough to predict its invasion.

## CONCLUSION

Anger is important to understand because it is a hindrance to emotional connection. Anger in any form hurts others and ends up hurting you by creating *dis*connection and taking away your ability to feel empowered. It is a reaction that everyone beyond infancy can do without and is useful only in the split second you realize it is present. The shelf-life of anger is less than five seconds. When you learn to identify those feelings and learn how to respond rather than react, the presence of anger in your life decreases immensely, and healthy and loving relationships become a reality.

Anger, however, is going to happen—within you and toward you. It is a reaction that exists. The good news is that now that you know anger doesn't work, you don't have to stay in the Reaction Box. You can get to the real issue and begin to experience the feeling of Empowered.

I am going to end this chapter with a story about Alicia, a thirty-five-year-old woman who was stuck in the Reaction Box.

Alicia was in a romantic relationship that seemed to be progressing, so she decided to relocate to be near her boyfriend. Two weeks before the big move, he disappeared. No calls. No text messages. No returned voicemails. She learned through friends that he had let his ex-wife move back in, and they had been seeing each other for the past four months.

Alicia was in therapy to get help with how angry she was feeling toward this guy. As you might imagine, her reactions (and emotions) ran high. Anger was keeping her safe, but the bigger issue was the obvious need to grieve, admit to feeling rejected, and the overall loss of a future with someone she loved.

We worked together to address where her anger was coming from, and she came to realize it was okay to grieve. Feeling rejected hurt but eased over time. She began to hope for a future with someone who could love her back. Alicia came to a place where she could face the outcome of her relationship and found acceptance of herself rather than seeking acceptance from others.

Just when she got comfortable in this new place of acceptance (empowering place to be), her ex-boyfriend contacted her and wanted "to see if they could still work something out."

Alicia's anger was back in full force. She pointed out that he had made no effort to acknowledge his behavior or how much he had hurt her. In one of our sessions, Alicia blurted out, "I am just so furious. What does he think I am, stupid or something? The nerve!"

Red Flag. I pointed out she spent the first thirty-five minutes of her session talking about him, his actions, and what he was doing wrong. We had spent time with her anger and what the presence of anger meant, so I directed her back to the Feeling Grid. She realized she was allowing anger back in, which meant she wasn't focusing on her true feelings. Her anger did not last five months this time, even though her wounds were wide open again. Within one session (or half a session), she began paying attention to the true emotion underneath the anger. Because of the work we had done in previous sessions, she could identify these feelings within sadness. He had hurt her, and she was sad.

By acknowledging her feelings and paying attention to her needs, she reclaimed what anger had taken away. She felt *empowered*. She texted him and told him how she felt. He had hurt her, and she no longer wanted to communicate with him. He acknowledged what she said, the text messages stopped, and Alicia got on with her life.

# ANGER EMOTIONS

| | TIER 2 | TIER 3 |
|---|---|---|
| **ANGRY** | Avoidant | Detached / Distant |
| | Defensive | Sarcastic / Exasperated |
| | Mad | Frustrated / Furious |
| | Selfish | Jealous / Envy |
| | Hateful | Resentment / Irritated |
| | Disgust | Appalled / Critical |

## Avoidant

**adj:** characterized by turning away or by withdrawal or defensive behavior

**The opposite of avoidant is aware.**

Avoidance on the Feeling Grid is an emotional reaction; we want to focus on the avoidance of emotion. Withdrawing from what you are feeling never works out in the long run. It might temporarily give some relief, but eventually, you will need to face the underlying emotion. Avoiding an emotion creates only more of that emotion in the future; for example, untreated sadness can turn into clinically diagnosed depression.

Relationally, when you avoid sadness or fear, that sadness or fear will be bigger when you do finally allow yourself to become aware of it.

## *Detached*

**adj:** standing by itself: separate, unconnected

**The opposite of detached is present.**

"That's it; I'm not talking about this anymore." Statements like that are an example of detaching. Maybe your spouse wanted to talk about setting up your wills and burial plans. We see this a lot with older couples. One spouse is a planner, while the other is not. Talking about death can feel scary or sad. To avoid this conversation, the non-planning spouse detaches emotionally. This prevents connection in the moment and creates distance in the relationship.

## *Distant*

**adj:** 1. separated in space: away;
2. separated in a relationship other than spatial

**The opposite of distant is close.**

Distant is the higher level or degree of avoidance. Becoming distant takes work; it takes action. When you detach, you begin to create distance between you and your sadness or fear. You disconnect, and distance only grows. The only way to reconnect with your emotions is to work to become more aware of what you are feeling.

## Defensive

**adj:** 1. serving to defend or protect;
2. devoted to resisting or preventing aggression or attack

**The opposite of defensive is intimate.**

"Push 'em back, push 'em back! Waaaay back!" Isn't that the cheer used across all sports? When you are defending yourself emotionally, you are pushing back and refusing to acknowledge the other person's feelings.

**Example:** If Bryan tells me I hurt his feelings, my instinct is to defend myself. I don't want to believe I hurt his feelings, so I defend myself, saying, "No, I didn't. I was trying to make sure you . . . ." In doing so, I ignore his feelings and then push onto him what I needed him to know: I am not mean.

## *Sarcastic*

**adj:** a sharp and often satirical or ironic utterance designed to cut or give pain

**The opposite of sarcastic is connected.**

Sarcasm is not just a sign of wit or humor; it can be a way of expressing and hiding your defensiveness. Exasperated displays defensiveness, while sarcasm hides it with humor. Similar to exasperated, sarcasm houses the reaction of defensiveness without committing to talking about what is truly being felt.

**Example:** About a year before Bryan's mom passed away in 2017, she joined our family on a trip to the museum. James and Isabel were ten at the time. At one point, the kids did something funny, but Bryan thought it was inappropriate and abruptly reprimanded them. The incident reminded him of being a kid with a strict, matter-of-fact mom. He made a sarcastic remark to his mom about being similar in his inability to be a fun parent. While he was still laughing at his comment, I glanced over at his mom and saw the hurt expression on her face. She felt the defensiveness in his tone and sarcastic reaction and was clearly hurt by the sarcastic comment.

## *Are you really joking?*

I had a thirteen-year-old client whose mom offered a dose of sarcasm each time the session ended, and we met in the lobby. "Well, did you fix him? He is one messed-up kiddo!"

The mom loved her son and was a very sweet parent, but their whole family used sarcasm in our exchanges. His dad would lob the same type of sarcastic question when he picked up his son from counseling: "Dang, I bet she had to work hard in there with you!"

Recognizing this pattern of communication, I decided to explore the effects of his parents' sarcastic remarks. I started by asking him if he knew the definition of sarcasm. "It's when someone says a joke, but it hurts your feelings," he said. He not only knew the definition—he felt it.

Sarcasm can be a fun way to communicate, but it can also be an anger reaction used to hide how you feel and defend your feelings. Every joke has a little bit of truth in it. Use humor for humor, not to defend your emotion.

# *Exasperated*

**adj:** having or showing strong feelings of irritation or annoyance

**The opposite of exasperated is caring.**

Similar to avoidance, but not quite mad, exasperated is a quiet way to react with anger. If you are exasperated, your reaction shows that you are not in agreement with something going on around you, even though you're not willing to talk about it.

**Example:** "Hey, Mom, I am going to let the kids get on the roof and help hang Christmas lights." "What?!" ("What?!" is Susan's mom's favorite exasperated reaction. And yes, it needs an exclamation mark next to the question mark because it comes out an octave higher than her normal voice.) When our three-year-old twins got on the roof with their dad to help him hang Christmas lights, she was exasperated because she was not in agreement. "What?!" was her way of saying she wasn't a fan of the idea. What it didn't express was that she was afraid for them.

## Mad

>**adj:** 1. intensely angry or displeased;
>2. affected by rabies
>
>**The opposite of mad is strong.**

Mad falls in the middle of the Tier-Two emotions because it is another way to explain anger. Mad is a bit of a no-brainer when it comes to defining it and being able to recognize it. (Unless, of course, you think you are affected by rabies. If you are also afraid of water right now, you might fall under the No. 2 definition of *mad*. Seek medical attention.) Mad is easier to understand by studying the differences in its Tier-Three emotions: frustrated and furious.

### *Frustrated*

>**adj:** feeling discouragement, anger, and annoyance because of unresolved problems or unfulfilled goals, desires, or needs
>
>**The opposite of frustrated is patient.**

Frustration is one of the most commonly expressed and mislabeled emotions and is a lesser degree of mad.

**Therapist:** "You sound like you were mad."
**Client:** "Oh, I wasn't mad. I was just frustrated."
**Therapist:** "So . . . you were mad."

Have you ever seen someone who is in a hurry while waiting for the elevator? The person rapidly pushes the already-lit UP button multiple times. Compare that person to the sweet elderly lady standing to the side, also waiting for the elevator. The rapid-button-pusher is frustrated. The opposite of frustrated is patient. The sweet elderly lady is what? Patient. When you are frustrated, you need patience.

Frustration doesn't seem like mad because it usually shows up for the *little things*, like a slow elevator. But what happens when multiple-button-pusher finds out the elevator is broken? Mad is right around the corner, and it might look more like the emotion known as Furious.

## *Furious*

**adj:** indicative of or proceeding from intense anger

**The opposite of furious is gentle.**

Furious is a higher level of an expression of mad. If you're furious, there is no denying that you're mad. It is a place most people don't want to be, but if you find yourself there, it is okay to admit you're furious. Just don't stay there. Recognize the emotion and use it to identify why you are furious and how to address or resolve the issue.

## Selfish

**adj:** concerned excessively or exclusively with oneself: seeking or concentrating on one's own advantage, pleasure, or well-being without regard for others

**The opposite of selfish is important.**

This is a difficult emotion to define and understand simply because selfish is used so commonly to describe others. It is important to distinguish between selfish and self-centered. Selfish is angry. Self-centered is getting caught up in yourself and forgetting about others. This is not malicious. There might be a place for being self-centered, not selfish. When I order food at a restaurant, I am centering on myself and ordering what I want; that's not a malicious act. If I decide everyone is going to eat what I am eating because it smells better and takes less time to cook, that is being selfish. There is no regard for the feelings of everyone else at the table.

Clients will say, "I am not going to share how much I am hurt because I am being unselfish." Actually, this is being selfish, because being authentic is the goal, and hiding your true feelings from the other person is only benefiting you. I want to know when I hurt my children's feelings. If I find out later, I feel that much worse that I hurt them. Selfish is a difficult emotion to recognize and will take practice. The best way to find it is usually when you begin thinking that you are the unselfish one.

**Example:** When our son began driving, he wanted to drive ninety miles away to visit his girlfriend. At first, I said no, explaining he had not had enough experience driving on the highway. After a few months of gaining some experience and confidence on the road, he asked again. I said no again, but this time, I realized my reason for doing so was more about me than his driving ability: I was scared to allow him to drive that far alone. The first time I said no, I did so out of parental concern; he needed to be a better driver to be safe on the highway. Saying no because I was scared, however, was a selfish reaction that I used to protect myself and that failed to take him into consideration. How does this connect to anger? My selfishness was also a form of avoiding due to my fear.

## *Jealous*

**adj:** vigilant in guarding a possession

**The opposite of jealous is validated.**

Jealousy is created when you are potentially losing something that is perceived as rightfully yours.

**Example:** An adolescent client was not talking to his stepbrother because he was jealous of him. The stepbrother got to have the client's dad as a basketball coach. The client struggled with seeing how much time his stepbrother was spending with his dad. He wasn't able to see how the stepbrother was learning and growing due to his dad's help in the new stepbrother's life, which was selfish. More specifically, he was jealous. His jealousy was understandable, but not talking to his stepbrother only created distance in their relationship.

## *Envy*

> **n:** painful or resentful awareness of an advantage enjoyed by another joined with a desire to possess the same advantage

**The opposite of envy is confident.**

Envy is created when you want or even feel entitled to something that was never yours.

**Example:** (Susan) My former graduate student took a job as an associate professor and started working toward becoming a full professor at her university. When she called to tell me she was granted tenure, my first feeling was anger, which surprised me. I loved this student. My immediate thought, however, was, *She didn't even thank me for helping her on her journey!* As soon as that thought crossed my mind, I knew that my anger did not make sense. The true feeling I was experiencing was envy. I was envious of her position because I had not attained that level when I was teaching. Selfishly, I focused on what I wanted, which kept me from connecting with her in a moment that was important to her.

Holding on to envy or jealousy can lead to becoming hateful.

## **Hateful**

> **adj:** 1a. intense hostility and aversion usually deriving from anger or sense of injury;
> 1b. extreme dislike or disgust

**The opposite of hateful is respected.**

Hate is intense, like Bryan's intense dislike of pimento cheese. When you hate something, it can be difficult to see any worth or redeeming value in it. (This is exactly how Bryan feels about pimento cheese.) Hate is not something we see frequently in counseling, perhaps because those who come to therapy are getting help before their anger intensifies into hate.

Clients are hesitant to view themselves as hateful or capable of feeling hate. They typically respond to the possibility with, "I don't know, hate is a strong word." We might be comfortable with hating objects, but when we use hate to describe how we feel about a person, we struggle. As strong as it sounds, it does exist in relationships. The important thing is not to deny our hate but to acknowledge that if we are expressing the following Tier-Three emotions we have connected to hate, others might be feeling hate from us.

Do you have strong feelings that can be described as hate?

## *Resentment*

> **n:** a feeling of indignant displeasure or persistent ill will at something regarded as a wrong, insult, or injury

**The opposite of resentment is gracious.**

The word that sticks out the most in the definition of resentment is *persistent*. When you are persistent, whatever you are being persistent with grows stronger. While anger creates a disconnect in relationships, harboring resentment fortifies hate and anger. There is certainly some overlap between resentment and the emotions of selfishness. Resentment arises when we don't get what we want, similar to jealousy and envy; however, resentment introduces the possibility of intentional harm toward the other person or oneself.

## *Irritated*

> **adj:** subjected to something that irritates; provokes impatience, anger, or displeasure in: ANNOYS

**The opposite of irritated is faithful.**

Irritated is a lesser degree of hate. It's bothersome, like an itchy tag on a T-shirt. You know the ones. You put on the shirt, and an hour later you remember how much the tag irritates your skin, and getting out of that shirt is all you can think about. Irritants can be big or small, but they do connect back to hate.

The opposite emotion of hateful is respected. The opposite of resentment is gracious. The opposite of irritated is faithful. Reflecting on these words provides insight into the anger reactions of hate, resentment, and irritation. It also reveals what is needed. When we hate, we are disrespecting. When we are resentful, we are not gracious. When we are irritated, our quick, potentially hurtful reaction fails to show faithful care for the other person or ourselves.

## Disgust

**n:** marked aversion aroused by something highly distasteful; repugnance

**The opposite of disgust is worthy.**

Disgust is a powerful emotional reaction that is used to make a point. If all forms of anger are used to avoid an emotion, consider how the power of the emotion of disgust parallels the degree of fear or sadness that is underneath.

The reaction is often immediate and seems almost involuntary. Disgust is identifiable across cultures. We turn our faces away, put up our hands, or spit out the objectionable food (like pimento cheese), and no one questions our emotion. The disgust is obvious.

Worthy is the opposite of disgust on the Feeling Grid. When you believe something is disgusting, you don't want to save it for later. It's not worth it, so you throw it out. Think about how that relates to the person (including yourself) or the relationship that disgusts you. Is that person or relationship worth saving?

## Appalled

**adj:** to become overcome with consternation (confusion), shock, or dismay

**The opposite of appalled is deserving.**

Based on the definition of appalled above, it might seem like appalled might be in the wrong location on the Feeling Grid. Confusion seems unsettled, not angry. But think about the person who is *appalled* and demands to speak to the manager! That person wants to share their disgust with a product, service, or experience. Appalled is a form of anger that is set apart by the accompaniment of shock or surprise. (Surprise is an emotion in the fear (green) box of the grid, which you will learn about in Chapter 6.)

## Critical

**adj:** inclined to find fault with severely and unfavorably

**The opposite of critical is admired.**

Critical comments can be a way of expressing anger while avoiding the real issue that needs to be addressed. Whether it's a thought about yourself, *I look terrible today,* or words or comments to others, "You shouldn't have gone this way," criticism is a form of disgust that can create a reaction of defensiveness. Do you see how anger creates more anger?

What about *constructive criticism*? If your goal really is to help rather than criticize, offer feedback instead of criticism. Feedback allows you to talk about yourself and your experience, whereas criticism focuses on the other person. Criticism is an anger reaction, and feedback is a response.

# GET EMOTIONAL

Anger doesn't work, but it has a purpose. Noticing your anger is the place to start developing emotional awareness. Keep a log of your anger over the next few days. Just anger. Don't worry about the other emotions. Take the time to be aware of how much anger you recognize. Track how often and what kind of anger you feel—frustrated, irritated, exasperated, etc. Pay attention to how you feel mentally, physically, and emotionally when anger shows up. For this exercise, it is not important to note with whom you are angry or to focus on the situation. The goal is simply for you to notice your anger.

## Going Deeper

- What is your anger imprint? Which words in Tiers Two and Three describe how you feel when you are angry?

- Think about a time when you felt angry. How did you react? How did your anger affect you or others in that situation?

- If you've struggled to recognize your anger, can you identify times when you've felt avoidant, distant, or detached?

- What underlying emotions might your anger be trying to cover?

# Anger
## Captured in a Quote

"Anger is never without a reason,
but seldom a good one."
—Benjamin Franklin

"Fools vent their anger, but the wise
quietly hold it back."
—Proverbs 29:11, NLT

"Anger is an acid that can do more harm to
a vessel in which it is stored than to
anything on which it is poured."
—Mark Twain

"How much more grievous are the
consequences of anger than the cause of it."
—Marcus Aurelius

"Anger and intolerance are the enemies
of correct understanding."
—Mahatma Gandhi

"Get rid of all bitterness, rage and anger,
brawling and slander, along with every
form of malice."
—Ephesians 4:31, NIV

# Sadness

> He who has felt the deepest grief is best able to experience supreme happiness.
> —*Alexandre Dumas, The Count of Monte Cristo*

**ON THE DRIVE HOME FROM SCHOOL, MY SON MENTIONED HIS FRIEND WAS BACK IN CLASS.** The boy had been out of school for a while because his dad had recently passed away.

"How is he doing?" I asked.

"I don't really know, Mom," James answered. "He was quiet all day, and I wanted to tell him how sorry I was that his dad died. But I didn't want to make him sad."

I had lost my brother to cancer quite suddenly a few months earlier and still felt the grief of that loss. I understood that James didn't want to remind his friend of his sadness, but I knew from personal experience that the sadness was there, regardless. And when nobody noticed, I felt lonely.

"You know, I have not forgotten that your Uncle James died. I miss him every day," I said. "I am willing to bet your friend has not forgotten that his dad died, either. When you ask how I am doing every once in a while, it feels good to share my sadness and talk about my brother. Your friend might feel the same way."

It can be hard to admit to or even acknowledge sadness. No one wants to ruin the moment by bringing up something that hurts. So we avoid talking about things that make us or others sad.

It's natural to think that sadness causes pain, but did you know facing sadness immediately decreases anger? Acknowledging the presence of sadness is what creates the possibility of feeling joy and peace. Why? Because it is impossible to experience joy or peace when anger is present. With that in mind, it's time to get to the emotions you have been avoiding for so long, starting with sadness.

We talk with clients every day who tell us they want to make their sadness go away. And then, there are the clients who refuse to acknowledge that they are sad or that they believe experiencing sadness is necessary. These perspectives of sadness are consistent across varying presenting problems: People do not want to be sad.

To help our clients, we need them to get to their *real* emotions, so we are all for sadness in session! We are ready for it with tissue boxes strategically placed around the office. When clients start crying during a session, they often apologize for the tears. Then, they apologize for needing a tissue. As if our preparedness with an abundance of tissues is somehow not for them. We buy tissue in bulk.

Some clients work hard to keep the tears from falling. Others are willing to talk about the people in their lives who are sad, acknowledging that it might be okay for others to feel sadness, but not them. We can relate to that! It is always easier to talk about sadness when we are not the ones who feel sad.

What about you? Are you comfortable being sad in front of others? Are you comfortable asking someone about their sadness when you notice it? Most people are not. Sadness, however, is part of the human experience.

Admitting to feeling sadness can also make us feel vulnerable as we share our authentic selves. When we refuse to admit to sadness, though, we aren't being honest with others or ourselves. Without authenticity—without being real with others—how can we connect within our relationships?

The truth is, we can't.

In the previous chapter, we explored the ways people use anger to avoid the emotions they don't want to feel, like sadness. In this chapter, we'll explain why people avoid sadness and why it is necessary to experience (or admit to feeling) this unavoidable emotion. We'll also equip you to handle sadness well. First, though, let's talk about why sadness is important.

## THE PURPOSE OF SADNESS

Have you ever broken your arm? It hurts! You can't just wait out the pain and hope the injury gets better on its own. Pushing through the pain and lifting weights to make your arm stronger would be counterproductive and do more damage. The only way to ensure a broken arm heals properly is to allow the doctor to stabilize the arm in a cast.

You can't ignore a broken arm, and it would be silly to try to hide that clunky cast. So you acknowledge the injury, give in to the cast, and invite people to sign it. Over time and with the right support, your arm heals.

The purpose of sadness is to initiate the healing process. Unfortunately, because people don't want to feel sad, the tendency is to ignore or avoid this basic emotion. The more you pretend everything is *fine*, the worse you feel and the weaker you become. That weakness evolves into anger, which then creates a disconnect between you and others. And this disconnect leads to more sadness and more anger.

If, however, you acknowledge sadness, your anger decreases, and you begin to heal with the support of others. In the process, your relationships have the opportunity to strengthen. It may sound risky, but we've seen this healing process in our clients' lives—and in our own.

When Bryan's mom passed away in 2017, he was seeing seven to nine clients a day. He wanted to continue working but wasn't sure how to avoid thinking about his mom while counseling. He decided to just be honest in session. He had lost someone he loved. Several years later, Bryan admitted that sharing authentically through the grieving process was therapeutic for him—and for his clients. I experienced the same pattern of emotion and hesitancy when my brother passed away in 2020.

It would have been inauthentic of us to pretend our sadness was not in the room after losing people who were so special and important. Acknowledging our sadness in the moment with clients seemed to encourage our clients that they could do the same, and we discovered that our therapeutic relationships improved. Neither of us had clients cancel or terminate because they thought we were weak or incapable; in fact, many of our clients said that our honesty increased their trust in us (strengthening the therapeutic relationship) and made them more willing to share their feelings.

Acknowledging sadness allows the healing process to begin. It frees you from having to pretend everything is okay. That freedom opens the door to experiencing hope, wholeness, and gratitude—feelings of joy.

> *Acknowledging sadness allows the healing process to begin.*

## The Lady in the Lobby

I (Susan) was waiting in the mechanic's lobby while my car got inspected when an older woman walked in. She moved slowly, with the help of a cane, and sighed heavily after she sat down. At first, I wanted to keep my AirPods in my ears because I didn't want to hear her complain or listen to an angry story. I solidified my excuse for not engaging with her by telling myself I needed to pay attention to the Audible notes I was listening to at the moment. Because I often talk about how much of the world we miss while we're looking at our phones, however, staying plugged in seemed hypocritical, so I put away the technology and decided to be present in the lobby.

After a few minutes, we made eye contact, and I noticed that she looked sad—or maybe tired. "Are you getting an inspection too?" I asked.

When she spoke, I didn't hear a trace of the anger I had assumed she was feeling. "Well, no. I have a dead battery. My car died in the parking lot of the grocery store, and I had to get a wrecker to tow it here."

I said I was sorry that happened and commented that it was a miserable situation.

She nodded and agreed that it was, but mostly because she was used to her husband taking care of the car. "I thought I had paid close attention to the lights on the dashboard, but then this happened."

I sat for a few seconds and then asked, "Did your husband pass away?"

She looked at me and gave with a short laugh. "Yes, but it has been eight years. This is the first time my car has broken down without him."

"Eight years is not such a long time, especially with this being the first time dealing with something like this without him."

The woman smiled and said, "Well, yeah," then looked down at her hands.

I paused before speaking again. "I think it seems like sad must be part of what you're feeling, no matter how long it had been."

Then she looked at me once more and said, "I lost a part of myself when he died."

"I can only imagine how hard it must be," I said.

The tech came in and told me my car was ready, ending my time with the lady in the lobby. Before heading to the register to pay, I told her I enjoyed talking with her.

"I have too. And you actually helped me," she said with a note of surprise.

I think she needed to hear it was okay to be sad. It seemed like she thought she shouldn't be sad after eight years. Recognizing her feeling as sadness made her feel better, which is the opposite of what you might assume would have happened.

The purpose of sadness is to bring healing, so why don't people want to share their sadness? Often, it's because they've bought into the myth that sadness is weak or admitting to being sad will make them feel worse. Leaning in and experiencing sadness does the opposite. It opens the door for feelings of joy.

> *Leaning in and experiencing sadness . . . opens the door for feelings of joy.*

## THE MYTH: SADNESS EQUALS WEAKNESS

From an early age, humans learn to gloss over sadness. Suck those tears back up into your eye sockets. Shut down the hurt—quickly—as if there is something wrong with feeling sad.

This practice is so ingrained that we don't realize what we are doing. Our son would come to us with tears streaming down his face, holding a broken toy in his hands. We would try to fix the toy, all the while telling him that he was fine and didn't need to cry. But he did. His sadness pulled us closer to him.

I remember once holding our daughter after she bumped her head, repeating, "You are okay," softly and lovingly. My mom said just as softly and lovingly to me, "She's not okay; she is crying." Such a valid point!

Why do we talk our children out of their tears of sadness? Because we want to teach our children to be strong, not weak. But sadly, we are all missing the boat. Admitting to sadness *is* the strength. Avoiding sadness lets anger rear its ugly head.

The myth is that sadness equals weakness, but the opposite is true. Being sad is hard.

If you, like so many of our clients, want to learn how not to be sad because you don't want to look weak, here's the secret: Be sad. Lean into what is hard and challenging. It's a sign of strength, not weakness.

One of our universal therapeutic goals is to allow people to feel and express their sadness. Heck, we welcome it with jazz hands when it shows up on our couch. As soon as a client talks about their sadness, the therapeutic relationship begins to strengthen and grow. Connecting through emotion increases, as does the authenticity in the room. With emotional honesty, we are better able to help our clients—and they are better equipped to help themselves.

Remember that You Are Here dot on the emotional map? Admitting to and sharing sadness is a wonderful way to connect because it allows us to understand each other and ourselves. Talking about what you feel helps you relate to others. Acknowledging that you are sad gives you the starting point on the emotional map that allows you to find ways to feel better. The only other option—and the one that people typically choose—is to get angry (distant or detached) because they are working so hard not to feel sad.

The bottom line is that if sadness exists, you have two options:

1. Admit the sadness and connect.

2. Or avoid the sadness and foster anger.

Feeling sad is more than okay. By reflecting on and sharing your experience of sadness, you can build trust and connectedness in your relationships and with yourself. That's not weak. That's true strength. The only weakness sadness creates is the avoidance of acknowledging it.

## PEOPLE DON'T WANT TO HEAR IT

The most common concerns we hear from clients when we encourage them to share feelings of sadness are . . .

1. They don't want to sound like they are complaining.

2. They think others don't want to hear about what's bothering them.

And these are not your superficial, easy-to-kick beliefs. They are hardcore, rooted-down-to-the-toenails beliefs. Where do these beliefs come from? Life.

Most of us have been told at some point to stop complaining. Not wanting to risk getting shut down or deemed a complainer, we refuse to acknowledge sadness. Most of us have felt overwhelmed at times, and we don't want to burden others with our problems. Fearing a reaction of irritation, hate, disgust, frustration, or avoidance, we deny, cover up, or try to pretend we aren't hurting. We get caught up in trying to predict how others might respond or whether they would be good at comforting before giving them the opportunity to help.

Choosing to be authentic in the moment requires facing the possibility of all those beliefs from the past: looking like a complainer, weak in front of others, or even not being heard or believed.

# THE TRUTH: THERE'S A RIGHT (AND WRONG) WAY TO SHARE

**Client:** "I tried that! I told her how I felt, but she didn't hear it. Sharing how I feel didn't work."

**Bryan:** "You are doing it wrong."

Exasperated clients sit on our couch and tell us they have tried talking about their feelings, but it didn't work. They didn't feel more connected; instead, they felt ignored, misunderstood, or hurt by the person with whom they had hoped to connect.

This is how emotional expression gets a bad rap. Too often, people think they are sharing emotion when they aren't. They may even use the words from the Feeling Grid and still miss the mark when it comes to sharing feelings. After all, if it were easy to share emotions, we would not have a continually full practice.

In other words, honing the skill of sharing your emotions is difficult and takes time and effort.

What we know for sure is that sharing and connecting through emotion *does work* if you do it the right way. So if the bottom line is that any hope of feeling better comes from recognizing and talking about sadness when it exists, how do you invite sadness into the room? How do you share your feelings the *right way*?

To answer that, let's start with an exercise. Consider the following sharing scenarios.

Someone you care about throws up their hands in frustration and directs one of these questions at you:

Why wouldn't you want to know how much my boyfriend has **betrayed** me?

Why don't you care about how much you **neglect** me and make me feel **lonely** when you look at your phone all the time?

Can't you see how **sad** I am and how much I am **grieving** the loss of my mom? I want you to know how **guilty** I feel about how I have treated you.

How would you feel if someone said those words to you (or shouted them at you) and you were the mother, husband, or boss? Chances are, you would feel attacked, accused, or criticized. Go back to the Four Rules of Communication in Chapter 2. How many of these rules are being broken in these statements?

When you state feelings but neglect to share emotion, it can sound like a complaint or a criticism, which tends to generate an anger reaction from the other person, *"Stop complaining!"* rather than garner the comfort you're seeking. That's because neglecting to share your emotion while stating feelings does not create a sense of emotional connection. Emotionless reactions come across as sarcastic, resentful, or frustrated—*angry*. And what does anger beget? Anger.

---

*Emotionless reactions come across as sarcastic, resentful, or frustrated—angry. And what does anger beget? Anger.*

---

Sadness can only be shared if anger is not present. Unfortunately, it often seems easier to use anger as a mask and simply react rather than to communicate true emotions in the moment. But reacting with anger and masking your sadness creates an emotional disconnect.

Let's look at those scenarios again, but this time, imagine someone sharing their emotion without anger:

Mom, I feel so **betrayed** by my boyfriend. I thought that this time, I could trust him, but I was wrong.

When you pull out your phone while we're at a restaurant to check the score, it makes me feel like I'm here by myself. I feel **lonely** and **neglected**, even though you're right here, and I know you care about me.

I want to do a good job on this project, but I feel so **ashamed** that I am letting you down.

Honestly, losing my mom last month was really hard. I'm still **grieving**, and it's hard for me to focus on my work—or on anything except for how **sad** I feel.

If you were the mom, husband, or boss in these scenarios, would your response be different for the second set of statements compared to the first set of statements? Would you be more receptive and less defensive, even if the comment wasn't what you wanted to hear? Notice also that the statements aren't attacking or judging the mom, husband, or boss. The focus is on the person who is hurting.

Remember, connecting with emotion depends on what you say and share, as well as what you don't say.

## WARNING: EMOTIONAL EXPRESSION SKILLS TAKE TIME

Emotional connection is a learned skill, and like any skill, it takes practice—both for you and for the person on the receiving end. Sharing your emotion for the first time, or the second and third, is not going to go smoothly. You might stumble over your words, not unlike the way someone using a new language while traveling in a different country might. Don't let a communication failure defeat your plan to learn to talk with emotion.

Keep the following rules of communication and practicing the language of emotional expression. Remember:

1. **It is a new skill**. You will fumble at first and will not be very good at sharing your emotions. Bear in mind it took more than one attempt for you to learn to walk, tie your shoes, or sing your favorite song.
2. **It is a new you.** The person you are sharing your newfound emotional language with might not recognize your new, emotionally authentic self.
3. **You're talking to another emotionally unskilled person.** The person receiving your authentic emotional expression might not know how to take it, especially if they haven't read this book and aren't privy to your plan to connect through emotion.

If you try to share your feelings, but it doesn't seem to work, keep practicing.

## CONCLUSION

Clients often ask, *How do I get rid of this sadness?* Or *When does the pain go away?* But that is not the point or goal of therapy. **We are not trying to eliminate sadness or fear**. These emotions are to be embraced as a part of who we are and what we experience. If you do not embrace your sadness, anger takes over. If you embrace your sadness, you allow yourself to look for joy.

Based on the Feeling Grid, the opposite of sad is joy, so the goal is to understand sad so you can begin to look for joy. When we're working with clients in their sadness, 100 percent of them report feeling relief or hope once they express sadness. When you start with sad in the Feeling Grid, the goal is to look for joy. Joy does not come to you; you move toward Joy. Revealing your sadness, loneliness, disappointment, shame, or feelings of worthlessness with the goal of finding joy seems paradoxical. But that is exactly how it happens.

Joy evolves from sadness, but it doesn't always happen quickly. Have you ever spent time with someone who has lost a child (of any age) or a spouse? This deep grief epitomizes sadness. Ignoring this emotional pain only makes it worse. So welcome sadness, even the hardest kind, because experiencing it is the only way to loosen its grip on you.

Sometimes, you have to begin the journey before knowing exactly how or when you will arrive at the destination. What if you start crying and can't stop? You will. What if you allow the pain and it overtakes you? It won't.

---

*Revealing your sadness, with the goal of finding joy seems paradoxical. But that is exactly how it happens.*

---

# SAD EMOTIONS

| | TIER 2 | TIER 3 |
|---|---|---|
| **SAD** | Apathetic | Indifferent<br>Numb |
| | Hurt | Disappointed<br>Betrayed |
| | Lonely | Abandoned<br>Neglected |
| | Despair | Grief<br>Dejected |
| | Guilty | Remorseful<br>Miserable |
| | Shame | Worthless<br>Inferior |

## Apathetic

**adj:** affected by, characterized by, or displaying apathy: having or showing little or no interest, concern, or emotion

**The opposite of apathetic is excited.**

Apathy is defined as the absence of emotion. How could the absence of emotion become an emotion? Well, first, remember that emotion always exists.* Emotions and feelings are pivotal in our ability to connect with ourselves and others. Not having that connection is inherently sad. Continued disinterest in things or activities is a symptom of depression.

Apathy can be the result of feeling hurt or lonely for an extended time. When people experience relentless pain in a relationship, they become numb. Indifferent and numb, the Tier-Three emotion of apathetic helps illustrate and identify the degree (or type) of apathy.

## *Indifferent*

> **adj:** marked by no special liking for nor dislike for something
>
> **The opposite of indifferent is enthusiastic.**

Indifferent is an emotion that expresses sadness with its lack of care. There is a difference, however, between feeling carefree and not caring about something (or anything). A few years back, I (Susan) had two family members in the hospital at once. Both needed help getting home and going to physical therapy. Both were going to be okay, but I was so lost (emotionally overwhelmed) that when asked a question, I responded, "I don't care." Will your brother need that walker to get to the car? "I don't care." The problem with indifference is that it shows *no* caring. I cared deeply about my family members, but in my sadness, it was as if I turned off my caring to conserve emotional energy. It's important to acknowledge indifferent as sadness so it doesn't move into anger.

## *Numb*

> **adj:** unable to think, feel, or react normally because of something that shocks or upsets you
>
> **The opposite of numb is passionate.**

Numb takes indifferent to the extreme and appears not to care about anything. The opposite of numb is passionate, an extreme kind of care that drives people to action. In contrast, someone who is numb might

---

* See "Emotion Exists" at the bottom of page 17.

see a potential solution to a problem and still be completely uninterested in doing anything to bring about a resolution. Numb can be the result of feeling emotionally defeated due to overwhelming feelings of sadness.

**Example:** A client came to counseling because she wanted to learn how not to feel so numb about her marriage. She believed she should be fighting to save her marriage, but she couldn't find the energy to care anymore. Reflecting on what led up to that feeling of numbness shed light on how she got there—and what she needed emotionally. For years, she had felt neglected by her husband and experienced disappointment after disappointment. Eventually, she stopped anticipating the possibility of something good happening in her marriage because it only led to more disappointment. This also led to resentment for her needs not being met and a belief that being critical of him would somehow protect her and inspire change in him. It didn't. Years of resentment, hurt, and criticism left her to protect herself and detach emotionally, which is feeling numb. What she discovered was that she needed to feel noticed and to start looking for the good things again so she could feel fortunate. In doing so, she experienced renewed passion for her relationship with her husband.

## Hurt

>**adj:** 1. injured or damaged;
>
>>2. mental or emotional distress or anguish

**The opposite of hurt is grateful.**

The parallels of physical pain make it easy to understand emotional hurt and its levels of severity. If you were dancing, and your dance partner stepped on your toes, would you tell him or her that they hurt you? If your toes were injured before the dance and your dance partner's clumsiness made the pain significantly worse, would you speak up or just keep dancing?

It would seem that telling your dance partner that you are hurt would make sense. He or she would probably apologize immediately and work hard to be more careful. Maybe they would choose a different dance step or offer to sit down and have a drink with you instead. You don't have to overthink it or prepare a talk. All you have to do to get your dance partner's attention is to say, "Ouch!"

For many of us, that "ouch!" comes involuntarily and instantly—and much more easily than the acknowledgment of emotional pain. When it comes to emotional hurts, it's as if we don't want people to know our emotional toes have been stepped on. But what if we exclaimed our emotional boo-boos out loud and in the moment? People could apologize quickly. Or if they chose not to apologize or even acknowledge that they hurt you, you would know not to *dance* with them again.

When people respond well to your admission of pain, you can reach to the other side of the Feeling Grid to feel gratified in yourself or grateful for those relationships. You feel appreciative because the apology is there and fortunate to have people who care about you.

Hurt needs to be addressed. Ignoring emotional hurts has the potential to increase and prolong the pain or lead to numbness. In the physical sense, chronic pain can desensitize people. When you live with pain for so long, you almost learn to expect it to be there and may not talk about the pain because you know people can't relate to it. In the emotional sense, chronic hurt can turn into apathy or anger and affect all your relationships.

The two extremes of the ways that we may be hurt are to feel disappointed or betrayed. If we're talking about toes, that's the difference between a misstep on the dance floor and someone stomping on your broken toe.

## *Disappointed*

**adj:** defeated in expectation or hope

**The opposite of disappointed is fortunate.**

Disappointed is on the mild end of hurt, and it is an emotion we've all experienced. We can be disappointed in a situation or with a person, and the feeling has to do with our expectations of how we want things to play out.

Parents might be disappointed with their kids for not doing what they were supposed to do. You might feel disappointed that you didn't get the promotion at work or that your friend forgot your birthday. You had hoped for one thing but got something you didn't expect or want.

## *Betrayed*

**adj:** treacherously mistreated, abandoned, or deserted

**The opposite of betrayed is appreciated.**

The most severe experience of hurt is feeling betrayed. Betrayal can take on many forms, from family or friends gossiping about you, a colleague taking credit for your work, or your spouse cheating on you. Emotional betrayal can cause serious injury to your ability to connect in relationships in the future. It is not an emotion to be taken lightly.

The phrase *taken for granted* comes to mind. This phrase carries a lack of appreciation with it as if you are abandoned, deserted, or not noticed. Is the person taking you for granted being intentional in expecting something and not acknowledging you? Maybe, maybe not. If you do not explore this feeling of betrayal, anger will begin to set in.

## Lonely

**adj:** 1. being without company;
2. sad from being alone;
3. producing a feeling of bleakness or desolation

**The opposite of lonely is whole.**

Feeling lonely is different from being alone. Alone is a physical state of not being in the presence of others. We can be alone but not lonely. Likewise, we can feel lonely in a crowd. Lonely is an emotional state in which we feel isolated, ostracized, or excluded. It is a very sad place to feel emotionally isolated. Lonely individuals need connection more than any other. When we connect, we feel whole (the opposite of lonely) or more complete.

Loneliness has two variations to allow specificity to the feeling: abandoned or neglected. Loneliness is often a response to how we relate or don't relate with others, and these two powerful words bring clarity to the emotional experience.

## *Abandoned*

**adj:** 1. left without needed protection, care, or support;
2. wholly free from restraint

**The opposite of abandoned is cherished.**

When someone feels abandoned, the loneliness is exemplified by the absence of someone or something that was once present. If you feel that the people in your life used to be more active and attuned but are now emotionally distant, you may feel abandoned.

## *Neglected*

**adj:** not given proper or necessary care or attention

**The opposite of neglected is noticed.**

Neglect is different from abandonment. With abandonment, someone has left, but with neglect there is presence. . If you have people in your life who do not attend to you or your feelings, you may feel neglected. Actively seeing and feeling someone neglect you is the difficult part. Feeling abandoned can be painful, but neglect can be just as detrimental because the person expected to offer concern and care actively withholds those basic needs in front of you. Abandonment is more passive, while neglect is more active.

## Despair

**v:** to lose all hope or confidence

**The opposite of despair is happy.**

You may be surprised to note that *depressed* is absent from the Feeling Grid. It was there early on because people liberally use the word *depressed* to describe their sadness. We kept the word there for a while and tried moving it around in the sadness grid to find the right placement for it, but it just didn't seem to fit. The more I (Bryan) learned about and explored emotional awareness with clients, the more clear it became that emotions are only experienced in moments—here for a short time before being replaced by another feeling. It's important to know that sadness is something that will happen but also that it does not have to linger.

In contrast, depression is a mood disorder that affects a person's functioning. Many feelings in sadness, including despair, can contribute to and be experienced when someone is depressed; whereas feelings come and go, depression is prolonged.

When clients describe their sadness as feeling depressed, it doesn't help me connect with them emotionally. It does, however, make me want to know more about how they feel and how long they have felt that way. The clinician in me starts to check whether they are meeting the criteria for this diagnosis. If clients truly are depressed, we certainly want to address that, but we also want to keep diagnosis and emotion separate. One way we maintain that separation is to encourage clients to be specific and accurate with their emotional expressions. This is where despair comes in.

*Despair* is a heavy word—a heavy feeling of sadness where all confidence and hope are lost. Isn't it comforting to know that emotions—even despair—come and go?

The Tier-Three feelings of this intense emotion, grief and dejection, help to illustrate and identify the degree (or type) of despair.

## Grief

**n:** deep and poignant distress caused by or as if by bereavement

**The opposite of grief is pleased.**

Grief is a commonly expressed emotion of despair that involves sadness based on loss. We all experience loss of some kind. Loss can take a variety of forms:

- The death of someone you care about
- A job loss
- Losing a memento, like a piece of jewelry that reminded you of something or someone special
- Loss of ability or functioning
- An empty nest
- The loss experienced when you move to a new town (even if it was a good move)
- A financial blow

Being able to recognize your sadness as grief over a loss helps you understand your emotions and why you are experiencing sadness. This specificity also helps others connect to your experience and perhaps even comfort you.

## Dejected

**adj:** low in spirits: depressed

**The opposite of dejected is elated.**

Dejected is a simple way to talk about feelings of sadness. Dejected also makes you think when you hear someone is feeling this way because of something you have done. Depression is tied to a diagnosis and can create less responsibility on the person feeling it or possibly causing it. Dejected is a more accurate description of emotion than the word depressed because it describes the experience in a moment. Dejected is a general term but specific in the way it feels. We do not use the word dejected often in our everyday vernacular. Perhaps we should. It is this specific generality that connects us back to despair and sadness and helps create clarity with others.

## Guilty

**adj:** 1. justly chargeable with or responsible for a usually grave breach of conduct or a crime;
2. aware of or suffering from guilt: feelings of deserving blame, especially for imagined offenses or from a sense of inadequacy

**The opposite of guilty is free.**

Guilt is the emotion that drives a person's thoughts about what they *do*. It is different from shame (the next Tier-Two emotion on the Feeling Grid), which is connected to how someone feels about who they *are*. These two emotions can coincide, but they are unique and are experienced and addressed differently.

When you feel bad about something you have done (or believe you are responsible for), you feel guilty. Guilt is a developed emotion, meaning you learn how to feel bad about your actions as you learn to recognize good from bad or right from wrong. Even so, the feeling is derived from within. You can't be "guilted" into doing something because this feeling has internal origins and is based on how you perceive right and wrong.

In many ways, today's culture has tried to remove guilt from the emotional playbook. The logic seems to be that individuals can do whatever they want without regard to how their behavior (words and actions) affects others. But that is not reality. What we do often has an impact on those around us—for good or ill. Failing to acknowledge that creates emotional disconnection.

Emotional connection takes into consideration how your behavior (words and actions) affects others' well-being. Guilt acknowledges the truth that we *can* do wrong. Without awareness of this feeling, we would lose the ability to connect with others. Purposefully avoiding or refusing to acknowledge guilt can destroy our relationships with others and ourselves.

The Tier-Three emotions remorseful and miserable illustrate the degree of guilt experienced.

## *Remorseful*

**adj:** motivated or marked by gnawing distress arising from a sense of guilt for past wrongs

**The opposite of remorseful is liberated.**

The acknowledgment of guilt often occurs because people feel remorseful or sorry for the way their actions impact others. When you feel remorseful, an apology is the first step toward receiving forgiveness and mending the relationship. An apology shows remorse and invites connection, both of which can liberate you from feeling the burden of guilt.

## *Miserable*

**adj:** 1. being in a pitiable state of distress or unhappiness;
2. wretchedly inadequate or meager;
3. being likely to discredit or shame.

**The opposite of miserable is delighted.**

Miserable is the internal experience caused by a heavy amount of guilt. The level of distress is markedly bad, probably because the guilt has been held within or gone unaddressed for too long. The more you hold onto guilt, the more miserable you will feel. While miserable is commonly used to describe everyday moments (the weather, traffic, or dentist appointment), it's important to recognize that this feeling word is connected to guilt. So maybe the weather creates a terrible moment, and the dentist creates a terrible feeling in your mouth. The root in miserable is misery, which is an intense level of sadness.

## Shame

> **n:** 1. a painful emotion caused by consciousness of guilt, shortcoming, or impropriety;
> 2. a condition of humiliating disgrace or disrepute
>
> **The opposite of shame is hope.**

Shame is the emotion or feeling about who you are. It is the little voice in your head that says *you are not good enough*.

Developmentally, we humans experience and understand shame before we learn about and grapple with guilt. The reason for this is that shame has an external component. It develops as we understand how (or *think* we understand how) we are perceived by others; for example, if you disappointed your parents, you might have felt shame. That understanding can come from words spoken by others or simply from our own thoughts.

Guilt stands on the shoulders of shame, which means even after you have resolved your guilt by offering an apology and making amends with someone, your negative view of self may linger. The apology could have been accepted, but you may not have resolved your shame.

Shame is one of the only emotions that has a distinct behavior associated with it: Shame hides, separates, and withdraws from relationships. Shame is so powerful that it crosses species. If I tell my dog, Boomer, that he is a bad dog (he really isn't—he is great), he will get up and leave the room because he feels shame. People respond similarly, which makes shame the antithesis of connecting.

The answer to resolving shame is simpler to say than it is to achieve. If shame puts us in the dark, then we need to shine a light on shame. We need to get specific about how we are feeling and why, and we need to test the words that the little voice in our head whispers to evaluate whether they are true.

The Tier-Three feelings of worthless and inferior bring the necessary specificity to the experience of shame.

## *Worthless*

**adj:** 1. lacking worth: valueless;

2. contemptible, despicable

**The opposite of worthless is proud.**

Worthless combines the noun *worth* with the suffix *less*, meaning without, but *without worth* does not fully describe the heaviness that comes with this emotion. When someone feels worthless, they may believe they deserve to be despised and merely worthy of contempt.

Feeling worthless is a frightening experience. This feeling is partly why the Feeling Grid exists because it can create so many other difficult emotions. Worthlessness travels with you when with people you love or when surrounded by strangers. It will show up everywhere in life: at home, in relationships, at work, or in your community. If you feel worthless, the simple act of acknowledging this emotion immediately creates enough light on the truth that you will feel some relief and begin to feel valued.

**Example:** A couple had been struggling to connect for years. The shift in their ability to hear each other and understand where the other was on the map of emotion came when the wife admitted how neglected she felt in the relationship. The admission seemed risky to her because she also recognized that her husband had always worked hard to provide all her needs and wants. The husband's response was epic—in the therapeutic sense. We had worked hard for the past several months with the husband's reaction of avoidance and shutting down, but in that moment, he began to cry. He just started talking. He felt worthless because his focus had been spent working to provide opportunities and beautiful things for his wife. He said he was proud of what he had accomplished financially, but now he felt stupid. He hated hearing that she felt neglected. He went on to explain how worthless he thought he was. The wife sat there watching her husband. Seeing him cry and hearing him talk about how he felt instantly created a connection. He said he didn't understand her response because he thought sharing how worthless he felt would lower his value in her eyes. The opposite happened. Expressing how he felt shifted their relationship and reestablished the connection that had been missing for so long.

## Inferior

**adj:** 1. of little or less importance or value;
2. of poor quality;
3. situated lower down

**The opposite of inferior is honored.**

It is never pleasant to feel inferior. This emotion can be connected to one's sense of self-worth, but it does not carry the weight of worthlessness. It's a shame emotion that comes from the belief that you are not meeting others' expectations. It denotes the sense that you lack standing or honor, the needed counter-emotion to the right of inferior on the Feeling Grid.

# GET EMOTIONAL

We have established that anger doesn't work and that we have to be willing to move in the direction of our sadness. This can be an incredibly difficult thing to do because nobody likes to feel sad. However, it is the one thing we need to be in order to find comfort and move toward joy. You are going to recognize your sadness, but will you be able to sit in it?

When we say *sit in it*, we mean that you need to not work to avoid or change this feeling. Allow the feeling to settle. Recognize what you are feeling. This requires a response and not a reaction. Take the time to notice if you are feeling either abandoned or neglected. Don't try to fix that situation, but rather know which one it is. The same can be said for any of the sad emotions. Be sad and maybe enact that Public Display of Emotion (PDE) Plan you learned about in Chapter 1 with others.

## Going Deeper

- What sadness do you most often cover with anger? What does your anger reaction say about your sadness?

- How successful were you at the PDE Plan? What was the other person's reaction to your authentic emotion?

- Have you believed the myth that sadness is a weakness?

- When others share their sadness with you, do you view them as weak?

- How does your shame limit you in relationships, jobs, or self-confidence?

- How can you comfort sadness in others? What type of comfort do you need from others when you are sad?

- Ask someone with whom you have expressed your sadness in the past what they thought of you for sharing.

# Sadness
## Captured in a Quote

"Sometimes it's easier to pretend you don't care than to admit it's killing you."
—*Unknown*

"I am both happy and sad at the same time, and I'm still trying to figure out how that could be."
—*Stephen Chbosky*

"Shame hates it when we reach out and tell our story. It hates having words wrapped around it—it can't survive being shared. Shame loves secrecy."
—*Brené Brown*

"Never despair, but if you do, work on in despair."
—*Edmund Burke*

"It doesn't hurt to feel sad from time to time."
—*Willie Nelson*

"Shame is a soul eating emotion."
—*Carl Jung*

# Fear

*The bravest are surely those who have the clearest vision of what is before them, glory and danger alike, and yet notwithstanding, go out to meet it.*
—*Thucydides*

**WHEN OUR KIDS WERE TEN YEARS OLD, WE TOOK A FAMILY TRIP TO CORPUS CHRISTI, TEXAS.** Susan thought she had scored a vintage remodeled hotel on Airbnb. She was correct about one thing, it was vintage, but it was not the best place to take your children. When we walked in, we each grabbed a child's hand and said, "Stay close." It was right on the water, and each room's sliding glass patio doors opened to the interior of the hotel, which opened up into a giant family-style area that included an indoor pool, ping-pong tables, foosball, billiards, and arcade games. We decided to stay and make the best of our situation.

We had gotten up early for a day of sightseeing, and while Susan was getting ready for the day, the kids and I headed out to the giant game room. James ran straight to the arcade games, where he began pumping coins into the machines at a steady pace. Isabel challenged me to a ping-pong match.

After losing a point in a heated battle of table tennis, I looked toward the arcade games to check on James.

He wasn't there.

I silently screamed, *He's gone!*

Trying to appear calm, I asked Isabel to pause the game. "Stay *here*," I told her before jogging to the wide hallway that led to the front desk where James and I had gotten quarters for the arcade games that morning. I saw a long line of people, but no James. As I ran back toward the ping-pong tables, Isabel was still standing at the ping-pong table with her paddle in hand, watching me run from one side of the room to the other. I grabbed her hand and then ran to the other side of the game room area, where some glass doors opened to the beach. I looked down the long sidewalk that bordered the beach. He was nowhere in sight.

Panic set in. Where could he be? How long has he been gone?!

That's when Susan walked up and saw my face. I could tell she saw the terror in my eyes.

She immediately performed the "count my chickens" mom scan for child one and child two. She saw Isabel standing by me with my hand in hers, and then, scanning the rest of the area, the fear on her face immediately matched mine. "Where is he?"

"I don't know," I admitted.

Continuing the search, I left Isabel with Susan. They ran back to our room to see if he had gone back there. I ran in the opposite direction, searching for my son.

Distraught and sweaty, I was running back to the ping-pong table and arcade area and saw him standing next to Susan and Isabel. Susan and Isabel found him standing alone where he had left in the first place, his arcade game. He had run out of coins.

Relieved and exhausted by the fear and helplessness that permeated my body for the last fifteen minutes, I grabbed the whole family and just held them all.

It took me a while to think straight again, but I was able to somewhat calmly ask James where he had been.

"I went to get more quarters," he said, "but when I got back, nobody was here. I didn't mean to be gone so long."

The look on his face told me he had experienced the same fear and helplessness I had felt. He said that he thought it would only take a few seconds, but there was a really long line.

He was standing in that long line that I perused too quickly and missed him. I hugged James again, my heart still pounding. "Just tell me where you're going next time, okay?"

That whole episode lasted about fifteen minutes, which isn't a long time in the grand scheme of things, but he's my son. So it was a long time. To this day (nine years later), I still remember the feeling of intense and undeniable fear.

This moment was the first time Susan saw me truly afraid—genuinely and authentically full of fear. We had been married for more than a decade by then, which is a long time for a wife to not see her husband's fear. The truth is, I had been afraid so many times since our wedding day. In fact, I experience fear every day, probably more than most. But just like most people, I was excellent at hiding my fear from others, especially my wife and my kids. I thought they wouldn't feel protected or that they might not respect me if I let my fear be part of our lives.

I want my loved ones to see me as all-knowing, relaxed, and trustworthy. In that moment, however, that moment I thought I lost my son, I couldn't hide or deny my fear. The fear of losing my son was so palpable that I could not deny how afraid I was feeling in the moment. It was also the beginning of my wife learning about me in a more authentic way, which helped us connect more in our relationship. Sharing my fear did the opposite of what I thought it would do. Susan didn't lose respect or feel less protected by me; she actually felt closer to me and more protected in our relationship.

## FEAR ISN'T ALWAYS OBVIOUS

I hid my feelings of fear from Susan for more than ten years without much thought or effort. Maybe I did not know I was afraid because I did not slow down long enough to define it. I can't say that I avoided fear throughout my marriage or in other relationships; I believe I grew up thinking afraid wasn't an option.

Fear is not always an obvious reason for what is happening in life or in relationships. In Chapter 1, we wrote about how we, as a society, tend to train our children to not be afraid. We want to keep on moving forward, making progress in life. We don't want to slow down. But it's often the fear of fear that slows us down.

Like sadness, fear is part of the human experience. It exists regardless of whether we call it by name. Even so, we have been trained to pretend fear is not there.

When clients exhibit fear, I'll ask them, "What is it that you are afraid of?"

---

*What are you afraid of?*

---

The typical response is paired with a look of confusion. "I'm not afraid."

Early in my career, I assumed clients' denial of fear stemmed from avoidance. Over the years, I realized my clients were not avoiding fear; the majority of them did not know they were even experiencing it.

How are we not aware of our own fear?

Simple. We normalize it and misdiagnose it.

Fear is continually more present than any other emotion. But wait, you say—anger is the most frequently used emotion. Yes, it is. People take ownership of anger before admitting to fear. Anger might be expressed and owned the most in society, but fear is present the most. The paradox with fear is that people talk about fear all the time yet never seem to be the ones experiencing it or taking ownership of it.

The dichotomy of fear being simultaneously normalized and avoided comes from living in a society that allows us to talk about fear without calling it fear. Confused? Maybe a few real-life examples of a client's experience will resonate with you.

## Confused Mom

A client sits in my office and expresses her worry, anxiety, and trepidation about her child starting school.

"What are you afraid of?" I ask, thinking this is the next logical question.

She gasped as if surprised and shook her head. "I am not afraid. I'm just nervous."

Worry, anxiety, trepidation, and even her response to my question, surprise, are all rooted in fear. Like most of my clients and Susan's clients, as well as most people, my client is describing fear.

When you look at the green box for Fear on the Feeling Grid, what word depicts *nervous* to you?

- She might feel *apprehensive* about letting someone else speak into her child's life.
- She might feel *confused* by the new daily schedule.
- She might feel *worried* that her child won't make friends.
- She might feel *vulnerable* as she hands over something so precious to her for safekeeping.

All of the italicized feeling words are emotional expressions of fear, and yet my client said she's not afraid. Emphatically, I might add.

In the previous chapter, we talked about the skill of emotional sharing and the fact that sometimes clients get frustrated and exclaim, "It doesn't work!" This example demonstrates the problem. When my client says she is "nervous," she is trying to talk about her feelings without actually expressing the one true emotion. She's talking about fear while denying it exists, which makes it difficult for others to connect with how she's really feeling.

When we share our feelings authentically and accurately, we can connect with others because they are able to find us on the emotional map. From there, we have the opportunity to work together to find the path that moves us from fear toward peaceful. And, spoiler alert, that's the purpose of fear.

## THE PURPOSE OF FEAR

Emotional awareness is where Bryan and I start most often with clients. You must understand how you feel before you can share those feelings effectively with others. Sometimes, people come to therapy because they are aware of their feelings but have no idea what to do with them. I also have a client who struggled with fear; I'll call her Beverly.

Beverly grew up in a home where she was not allowed to express emotions. The environment she described was consistently a *Suck it up, and you'll be fine* mentality. She had learned how to hide her feelings—especially sadness and fear. As an adult, she continued to keep her feelings to herself. A poised and professional woman, Beverly didn't want to risk being viewed as *emotional* or *overly sensitive* at work. Not surprisingly, her emotional tank became overloaded and full to the brim with stuffed emotions. There was nowhere else to hide her emotion, and she was afraid her emotions would seep out in front of everyone. She began to experience panic attacks at work.

In one of our sessions, Beverly said, "I'm afraid to go to work. What if I have another panic attack?" She feared that her coworkers would think she was weak and not in control of herself if they witnessed her having a panic attack. The simple fact that no one in her office knew about her anxiety added loneliness to the list of emotions she didn't want to feel.

"What if you told someone at work about how you're feeling?" I asked.

Beverly shook her head. "There's no way I can talk about this with anybody at work."

"No one? Is there anyone at work you could trust?" I asked.

She thought for a moment and then told me she had one coworker who was a family friend. "But we don't really talk much," she said. "At least not about anything personal."

As we closed the session, I said, "I know it might not be easy, but if you share with your friend how alone you feel and that you are afraid of losing credibility if you have a panic attack at work, it could ease up that heavy feeling of having a panic attack."

When I saw her the next week, she told me she had done just that. "I went into my friend's office, closed the door, and, well, I told her what was going on with me," she said, "and I immediately felt this sense of relief and that I was not alone."

Beverly had shared her feelings of loneliness and the fears she had about her anxiety. It turned out that she wasn't as alone as she had believed.

"As I was talking, my friend started to cry. She told me she had experienced a lot of the same feelings of anxiety and being alone at work with it."

"How did that feel—the moment you realized your friend heard your sadness and shared hers?" I asked.

Beverly smiled. She told me they had talked several times throughout the week, which made her feel less alone. The panic attack she feared seemed less likely, and her overall anxiety had decreased that week.

## Fear Can Cultivate Bravery

We avoid fear because it makes us look like we are weak and not brave. But the reality is that acknowledging fear will cultivate bravery. Fear has to be acknowledged, though. Fear is our ally if we accept its presence. Beverly was so afraid of having a panic attack she dreaded going to work. The one thing that made her fear begin to dissipate was acknowledging it—first to herself, then to me, then to her friend at work. Did it take courage? You bet! Courage can't exist without fear. Everyone experiences fear, so obtaining bravery is simply a matter of whether one decides to acknowledge the fear. What happens when fear is not acknowledged? Anger sets in. Bravery requires an acknowledgment of the presence of fear and then a willingness to act in spite of it.

Notice, too, that it was when Beverly admitted and shared her fear that she was able to find relief in her anxiety. Identifying your fear allows you to find your bravery.

---

*Identifying your fear allows you to find your bravery.*

---

If you are fearful of driving through traffic and bad weather, then checking the weather and traffic report is a recognition of that fear. Pretending that you are not scared leaves you unequipped to deal with that fear. Being aware of our fear allows us to prepare for or even potentially prevent a negative outcome.

When Beverly found the courage to talk to her coworker, she experienced an empowering emotional connection as well as some relief from her anxiety. Neither of those things would have happened if she hadn't acknowledged and shared her fear of having a panic attack. No one even knew she was hurting or afraid—how could they? She had worked hard for years to hide her emotions from everyone. Nobody is going to think to walk up to Beverly and ask if she is afraid; that's not something that is acceptable in society. As a rule, people don't go around asking others if they are afraid.

Think of it this way: Imagine being a parent of a toddler and training them to sleep through the night. One night, while your toddler is sound asleep, you tiptoe into your child's room and find her sound asleep. Now imagine waking up your sleeping two-year-old to see if she is having a bad dream. Confused, your toddler says no, or more likely, starts crying because you woke her from a peaceful sleep. You console her and get her back to sleep. An hour later, you tiptoe into the room again, wake your sleeping child, and ask, "Were you having a bad dream?"

As ridiculous as that scenario sounds, that's what we expect of others when we don't talk about our fear or sadness but want them to know how we feel. We want people to comfort us, but we don't want to talk about the fact that we need comfort. We avoid being afraid.

Fear serves many purposes, such as growing bravery, but the most important and basic feeling it pushes us toward is peace. Peace is what Beverly felt when she acknowledged her fears and shared them with her coworker. If we don't acknowledge our fear, we cannot use it to work toward peace.

## BUSTING THE MYTHS ABOUT FEAR

As with all other emotions, talking about our fear allows us to connect with others. Fear can feel debilitating, overwhelming, simple, silly, surprising, and demoralizing. Everyone deals with fear, so why is it that we don't want to talk about it? In the story we shared about losing James at the hotel, Bryan mentioned he wanted us to see him as all-knowing, relaxed, and trustworthy. Avoiding fear has become normalized in society due to all the myths surrounding it. Bryan's not ever showing fear as a strategy for being strong and trustworthy in the eyes of his family is built on a myth, one of many that involve fear. Let's explore a few and see which ones resonate with you.

## Myth: Fear is weakness.

**Truth:** Fear is not weak; it is a feeling. Period. Just like with sadness, what you choose to do with your fear determines how much control and what effect this emotion has over your life. Ignoring fear and not allowing fear is what creates weakness; leaning into fear is what helps you grow strong.

Perhaps it is the involuntary physical reactions caused by fear that allow this myth to persist. The instinctive fight, flight, or freeze responses leave us with the sense of being out of control. We pace, jump, scream, or run away—all without thinking. Sometimes, we lose the ability to speak. Other times, our body movements may increase as a way to cope. Are you a nervous fidgeter? Do you pace while on the phone? Maybe you just bounce your foot while seated?

We dismiss our fear because we assume that acknowledging it shows weakness. We deny fear because we believe that naming it for what it is will give the emotion more control over us. The truth is that how we deal with fear is what displays our courage and bravery. Choosing to acknowledge fear and share our feelings with others takes far more strength and courage than hiding or denying it.

## Myth: People can't understand my fear, so sharing how I feel wouldn't matter.

**Truth:** The commonality that all people share is the knowledge and past experience of fear. It is the detail of what makes a certain person afraid that varies. Someone may not understand the "why" of your fear, but everyone does experience fear. It is unfair to expect people to understand or experience the same fear you do or vice versa. When we talk about connecting with someone through emotion, we are not stating that you must understand the other person's fear. You simply have to *acknowledge* that they feel fear.

Trying to *understand* (make sense of or agree with) someone's fear can be counterproductive because it takes the conversation out of an emotional context and tries to force it into a cognitive context. In Chapter 3, I (Bryan) mentioned Susan's fear of cockroaches. I don't understand that fear—particularly if the bug is dead, on its back, and unmoving under a couch ten feet away. That said, whether I agree that Susan's fear of cockroaches is rational is irrelevant. The point is simply that I acknowledge she feels fear when she sees one of those crunchy brown critters. That's it.

Acknowledging someone's fear is what opens the door for connection. Regardless of whether you share someone's fear or have ever experienced the same kind of fear, you can understand what it means to feel afraid, and that's all that matters.

When I hear that my wife is afraid, the circumstances don't matter. The emotion she is experiencing is what is most important to me. Acknowledging her fear of that dead cockroach means that I don't try to talk sense into her by arguing that spiders are way more scary (but they are, right?). I simply grab a paper towel, retrieve the dead cockroach from under the couch, and smash it in the paper towel to assure her of its demise. That is all she needs to feel comforted in the moment.

## Myth: People don't need me to tell them I am afraid.

**Truth:** Oh yes, they do.

It's nearly impossible to predict with accuracy what someone is afraid of unless we are told. Recognizing someone's fear can be equally difficult.

Heck, we aren't great at recognizing our own fear! We all feel fear, but we do not all share the same kinds of fear, nor do we experience fear the same way. Your husband needs help knowing when you are afraid. Your boss could benefit from knowing if you are hesitant because your child is sick. Your best friend could use some help understanding why you keep avoiding her. While we might need to do the opposite with our children, asking if they are afraid when they shut down or hide in their room, this is role modeling and teaching them to talk about their fears.

If you refuse to share your feelings of worry or concern, others may be able to tell that something is bothering you. They just won't know what it is. If you are distracted at work because you are worried that you might have left the iron on that morning, others may notice that something is *off* (not the iron). Unless you talk about what you are feeling, they will have no idea why you are disengaged or distant.

Here's where things go downhill fast: If people perceive your *off* mood and lack of communication as anger (detachment) rather than fear, they may assume you are mad at them and respond with anger in the form of a reaction of resentment or defensiveness. In response to their anger reaction, you protect yourself by being emotionally distant. Before, you were just worried, now you're angry and doubting your coworker's loyalty. You begin to spiral and think: *What if he's after my job?* Now, everyone is operating in the Anger Box with one another! And it's all because you refused to acknowledge that you were worried about whether you left the iron on.

It would be much simpler to say, "I'm worried that I left the iron on this morning."

To which your coworker might respond, "Well, run home and check. I'll cover for you."

Worry resolved. Anger averted.

Now you can relax and get back to work.

## DON'T TELL ME NOT TO WORRY

**Mom:** "Just don't worry about it."

Kid (age eight to sixty-eight): "How is that even possible?"

As much as moms everywhere would like us to turn off worry, it doesn't work like that. Worry is an emotional expression of fear, and it has a purpose. Still, an underlying belief persists that people should not worry.

We hear this belief repeated by clients who heap this shaming language on themselves as the solution to their anxiety. "I shouldn't worry!"

We usually respond playfully with, "I guess that fixes it!" (If only people discovered the just-don't-worry solution sooner. Then no one would ever worry!)

Of course, telling yourself not to worry doesn't fix anything.

Why, then, from Bob Marley to Bobby McFerrin to moms everywhere, is there such a push against this feeling?

The message is well intended. When someone tells you not to worry, what they are really saying is that they don't like to see you wrapped up in fear. They're right: Letting worry consume your life and allowing it to keep you from living it is not a good thing.

Worry doesn't have to consume you. It can even be the thing that makes you pay attention to what matters to you.

I worry about my kids driving to school.

I worried about doing well in school.

I worry about that limb that hangs over the house.

What do all three of these worries have in common? They are about people or things I care about.

I care about my children and their safety.

I cared about doing well in school because I knew it would help me be successful and better prepared for my career.

I care about my house and that limb possibly damaging the house.

Worry expresses care.

So if worry expresses care, and you tell me not to worry about something I've just shared with you, what I hear is, *Don't care about that*—which is not only impossible but also disregards how I feel.

In Chapter 2, we talked about the need to listen for emotional expressions. When someone says, "I'm worried about . . ." don't be so quick to dismiss that person's admission of fear. Hear the meaning behind the words: *This is important to me.* Listening to someone doesn't mean you are worried about the same things. It means you care about that person.

## IS FEAR STANDING IN YOUR WAY?

When Susan and I work with clients, getting to the underlying emotion is the goal. When fear is in the mix, it can dominate a person's behavior and prevent people from addressing other emotions. In other words, unchecked fear can block your path to getting what you need. That's exactly what was happening for my client, Virginia.

Virginia had come to counseling previously with her husband, Stanley. This was a second marriage for the both of them, and some of their ability to connect seemed to be missing. Virginia came back for individual counseling to discuss the sadness she felt in the relationship.

Stanley worked until seven on weeknights. By the time he got home, Virginia had already eaten dinner and settled down in their bedroom to watch television. He would take his plate and retire to his office, working on his computer for the next several hours. Meanwhile, Virginia watched television until she fell asleep alone.

Deeply hurt by the neglect and loneliness she felt in the marriage, Virginia's anger kicked in. They had learned about emotional sharing in couples counseling, so she tried talking to Stanley. Unfortunately, she fell into the trap of talking about everything except herself and how she felt. She broke all four rules, telling Stanley what he was feeling, what he was thinking, and giving him advice on how to be better at their relationship. She continued her communication failures by listing all of the ways she believed he was failing her as a husband and causing her to feel lonely and neglected.

You can imagine Stanley's reaction to her criticism. From his point of view, he was working hard to earn a living to take care of her. The inadequacy he felt as a husband, combined with the hurt at her lack of appreciation, came out in a rage of loud, ugly words.

When things finally calmed down between them, Virginia was afraid to approach Stanley again. She resorted to maintaining the peace (which wasn't really peace, but silent disconnection) by keeping her feelings to herself.

During one of our sessions, Virginia told me she had finally given up trying to talk with Stanley about her sadness. "I can't handle feeling lonely and his anger at the same time. I know that if I bring it up again, he'll just lash out like he always does," she said.

Sadness was the issue in the relationship, but fear stood in her way. I knew that before she could address sadness comfortably, we had to address her fear. As we talked through both emotions, I asked her what she was most afraid of in the relationship. Her twofold answer revealed several fear emotions. She dreaded another angry response that would just add to the sadness. His words hurt as much as her loneliness. She also feared that if she pushed him too hard, she would push him away. The fear of being rejected in another marriage and having Stanley abandon her kept her from speaking up about her sadness, which made her feel helpless to change her circumstances. Then we talked about the skill of sharing emotion—how to share *with* emotion rather than talk *about* it and how to relay her true feelings rather than hedge the issue by casting blame and focusing on things he was doing wrong.

The following week, Virginia told me Stanley had come home early that Friday. They were enjoying the cool spring evening with a drink on the patio but, per usual, were not talking. Remembering our conversation, Virginia looked at Stanley and said, "I have something I need to talk to you about, but I am so afraid that you are going to respond with anger. I don't know what to do about it," she said.

Stanley turned toward Virginia and calmly said, "I promise you that I will not get mad."

From there, their conversation put them on a path toward resolving the sadness and hurt between them—a path toward peace.

Were all their issues resolved in that one conversation? No. But it was a start, and the more they practiced sharing their feelings honestly, the better they got at it.

The same can be true for you. If fear is standing in your way, acknowledge it. Call it by name. Make it your ally instead of your adversary. Fear is not the enemy; it's the gateway.

> *If fear is standing in your way, acknowledge it. Call it by name. Make it your ally instead of your adversary.*

## CONCLUSION

Fear is fearful. The myths and biases related to fear can seem a bit daunting. This chapter has highlighted a need to move in a different direction: We must allow ourselves to be afraid. The desire to understand our fear or be understood is the problem with the way that we typically handle fear. The whole premise of wanting to be understood violates the Four Rules of Communication. You are making the focus on the person you are talking with rather than sharing about yourself. You cannot force others to agree and understand what you are feeling. They can only hear it. Perhaps you get lost trying to justify or rationalize your fears with yourself. The simpler path is just acknowledging fear.

If we need to work toward peace, then it must begin with acknowledging our fear. Acknowledgment leads to an infinite number of avenues for us to achieve, surpass, and conquer the challenges in our lives. It is not always about sharing our feelings. Sometimes, the best thing we can do is know that something is fearful so we can make the right decisions to eliminate that fear. This is a more productive way of protecting ourselves than anger. In fact, this method works!

Comfort comes from others, but at times, we are the ones that bring our own peace. It takes work to be comforted because we have to do the first step: admit, own, acknowledge, confirm, reveal, or accept that we are afraid. This is the path to peace.

# FEAR EMOTIONS

| | TIER 2 | TIER 3 |
|---|---|---|
| **FEAR** | Concerned | Confused / Embarrassed |
| | Rejected | Insignificant / Inadequate |
| | Scared | Discouraged / Exposed |
| | Helpless | Vulnerable / Useless |
| | Dread | Surprised / Apprehensive |
| | Anxious | Overwhelmed / Worried |

## Concerned

**adj:** 1. anxious, worried;
2. interestingly engaged

**The opposite of concerned is supported.**

*Concerned* is one of our favorite emotions to express. As parents, we have ample opportunity to feel concerned:

"I'm concerned about your grades."

"I'm concerned that these friends of yours are not very friendly."

"I'm concerned that you think spending that much time playing video games is okay."

Parents are concerned!

It's important to recognize that *concerned* sits right below *disgust* on the Feeling Grid. If your underlying emotion is concern but you express disgust, your child will feel the anger. To communicate concern effectively, consider the Tier-Three emotions confused and embarrassed to bring specificity to what you're feeling.

## *Confused*

**adj:** being perplexed or disconcerted

**The opposite of confused is nurtured.**

Confusion is an uncomfortable experience and tends to be one that we seek to remedy quickly. This state of disorientation is resolved with clarity, which means asking questions. Sometimes, those confused questions sound like criticism (anger): *why, what,* or *how on earth?!* Confusion expressed as anger (critical) invites an anger response. Confusion expressed authentically invites support. The next time someone tells you they are confused, use your emotional awareness skills and hear their fear and not their criticism.

## *Embarrassed*

**adj:** feeling or showing a state of self-conscious confusion and distress

**The opposite of embarrassed is reinforced.**

No one likes to feel embarrassed, but we all do from time to time—even if we try our best to avoid embarrassing situations. Embarrassed expresses a feeling of concern in that it is a fear of criticism or rejection mixed with self-conscious confusion.

Early on in the building of the Feeling Grid, we struggled with the placement of embarrassed. People do not usually connect being embarrassed with fear, but that is what it is—not a higher level of fear, but similar to confusion and slight distress. If what you are embarrassed about intensifies, disgust could grow if ignored or a feeling of rejection could surface—feelings that are on either side of embarrassed.

## Rejected

**adj:** not given approval or acceptance

**The opposite of rejected is accepted.**

This emotion is often confused with feeling hurt. While rejection might lead to feeling hurt, it is the fear of rejection that places it in the Fear Box. If we are feeling inadequate or insignificant in a relationship, we are more than likely experiencing rejection.

## *Insignificant*

**adj:** 1. lacking meaning or import;
2. small in size, quantity, or number;
3. not worth considering: unimportant;
4. lacking weight, position, or influence: contemptible

**The opposite of insignificant is significant.**

When someone feels as if their input or approach makes little difference or is unimportant to others, then they may feel insignificant. The lack of consideration is a rejection. This emotion's placement next to embarrassed reveals the connection between rejection and embarrassment.

## *Inadequate*

**adj:** not enough or good enough: insufficient

**The opposite of inadequate is acknowledged.**

If we are not able to meet the needs or expectations, either of ourselves or from others, we may feel inadequate. We can manage this feeling by choosing not to compare ourselves to others or set unreasonable expectations of ourselves. This might be unrealistic because, as humans, we do compare, and we do strive to do more (or end up doing more) than we can handle. Feeling inadequate is not the problem because we all feel inadequate at some point in time. Not admitting feeling inadequate is the problem. If the pilot of my airplane feels inadequate I would really like him/her to speak up! Micromanagers in a company are a good example of this. Is there anything wrong with needing help? Is there anything wrong with not meeting all expectations? No. Hiding these feelings is what creates the downfall.

In the moments we fear being inadequate or rejected, maybe all we are looking for is that we are doing okay and are accepted.

## Scared

**adj:** thrown into or being in a state of fear, fright, or panic

**The opposite of scared is loved.**

Synonymous with afraid, this Tier-Two emotion can be hard to admit. When people ask, "What are you afraid of?" or "Are you scared?" the common but dishonest answer is "nothing" or "no!" Admitting to being scared, however, allows us to seek encouragement and protection by sharing our feelings with people who can comfort us.

Scared is not cowardly! It is acknowledging the presence of possible danger or challenge that you are facing. Admitting to being scared promotes survival and protection. You may not be as well-versed in Texas History as I profess to be, but the way I look at the exploits of General Sam Houston, the commander of the Texan Army, is that of recognizing that he is scared.

The Mexican president, Santa Anna, had a command of 5,000 troops compared to General Houston's 910 men, who were basic citizens converted to military men. General Houston continued to retreat, knowing his army was outnumbered five to one and no match for a standard assault. General Houston believed in Texas, but he was also scared of losing another battle to Santa Anna. The battle cry of "Remember the Alamo" was born that fateful April day at the Battle of San Jacinto, with the perfect geography, timing, and some aid from spies in the camp. Being scared became tactical, but also preserving. General Houston's army won the battle mainly because he knew when to admit he was scared. Admitting scared was strategic, not cowardly.

## *Discouraged*

**adj:** 1. to deprive of courage or confidence: DISHEARTEN; 2. to hinder by disfavoring

**The opposite of discouraged is encouraged.**

Discouraged can be a valid feeling based on how others are treating you, or it can be based on your own self-talk. For whatever reason this feeling exists, you need to recognize it and talk about it. The hope is that recognizing this information is useful in being able to move in a direction that is more encouraging.

Susan owned a Jeep Wrangler when we were first married. She, being the more laid-back one of the two of us, never put the top back on in time when the storm clouds rolled in. Oftentimes, I had wet pant legs when I walked into work due to the water sloshing around in the bottom of the jeep bed. You can imagine my discouragement when I heard it raining in the middle of the night. I could have complained and listed my frustrations, but that wouldn't help. When I shared the inconvenience of all the rainwater and asked if I could help with keeping it dry, she realized how I was affected and worked to put the top back on in time. She even researched how to get the water drained. *Who knew there were plugs for water drainage in the bed?* I think my encouraging her, as opposed to being discouraged toward her, created a sense of confidence in her.

## *Exposed*

**adj:** 1. open to view;
2. not shielded or protected

**The opposite of exposed is protected.**

Feeling exposed is a unique and exact term for scared. My first thought is streakers and flashers. They don't seem scared. Of course they aren't; their act is planned. We equate being exposed to the fact that others might know how we are feeling or see something about us that we don't want them to see. Again, it is not about feeling exposed. It's admitting the feeling of being exposed and what we do in the moment that's important. Do we move back into anger, or do we admit to feeling exposed?

I went on a hiking date in college. We arrived at Palo Duro Canyon State Park late in the afternoon. I was way more focused on my date than that necessary amount of fear you need hiking to stay safe. We were still out on the trail when the sun began to go down, and we were in the second-largest canyon in the United States. And I had lost the trail. As the temperature dropped and visibility decreased, I prayed that the moon would be bright. Talk about feeling exposed! I did not want my date to know that I was failing as an Eagle Scout. I had talked up my ability as a hiker and the ease I could provide if she agreed to go. I felt so exposed and open to criticism! Finally, I tracked us back to the trail, thank goodness, and was thankful for my dad's pushing me to become an Eagle Scout.

## Helpless

**adj:** 1. lacking protection or support;
2. marked by an inability to act or react;
3. not able to be controlled or restrained

**The opposite of helpless is secure.**

When we feel helpless, it seems as if all our efforts lead to nothing. It's a feeling of being out of control and unable to do anything to change our circumstances. Many people feel as if they have no control over their lives or situations. They feel stuck and are uncertain about what will happen next. If helplessness persists, it can lead to dread regarding the future. The two identifying emotions of helplessness are vulnerable and useless.

## *Vulnerable*

>**adj:** 1. capable of being physically or emotionally wounded;
>   2. open to attack or damage
>
>**The opposite of vulnerable is safe.**

Similar to the experience of being *exposed*, vulnerability leaves us feeling as if we are open to an attack. Nobody likes to feel vulnerable because it means we could be hurt either emotionally or physically. Being vulnerable, however, does not mean that we *will* experience attack or pain, only that we might. The uncertainty associated with vulnerability can also leave us feeling helpless.

## *Useless*

>**adj:** 1. having or being of no use;
>   2. ineffectual;
>   3. not able to give service or aid.
>
>**The opposite of useless is trusted.**

Useless could be a fact; for example, a cup with a hole in the bottom is useless or ineffective for holding liquid, and there is nothing the cup can do about that. When someone describes themselves as feeling useless, they are expressing a similar thought: They are struggling and can't fix the situation or the problem on their own. I have felt helpless before, and it seemed like every effort to gain control of the situation only created more issues. Recognizing your useless feelings is, in fact, working toward finding the solution to your problem. Whether it is admitting you need to change directions or you need help, both options support growth.

# Dread

**n:** great fear, especially in the face of impending evil

**v:** 1. to fear greatly;
2. to feel extreme reluctance to meet or face

**The opposite of dread is assured.**

Dread might not be a word you use every day, but you know it when you feel it. It can be an intense fear that comes when you're waiting for a medical diagnosis or something more mild, like the discomfort you feel when you unexpectedly have to rearrange your schedule on a busy day. Or it might be how you feel knowing you are obligated to attend an event or have a difficult conversation. The surprise or apprehension of something you don't want can fill you with feelings of dread.

## *Surprised*

**n:** the feeling caused by something unexpected or unusual

**The opposite of surprised is relieved.**

Surprise on the Feeling Grid is different from surprise at a birthday party or a surprise attack. We are talking more about being surprised with information that you were not prepared for. Let us say you heard some news that changed everything about your plan for the day. It does not have to be dooming news, just a change of plans. There is the initial shock that changes the plan, followed by the need to make new plans. Surprised by the turn of events, you regroup while muttering, "It's okay. It's okay. I can do this."

Sometimes, silence occurs when we are surprised. I had a client who was going through a divorce. This was both a sad and fearful time in his life. In particular, it seemed like his ex-wife would change things on him rather abruptly. The constant changes created a silent reaction from him. His wife used the silence to find fault in him as someone who was "angry at anything she told him." I provided a little empathy in the moment and shared that it seemed more like all the changes were a surprise to him, and he might be caught off guard and surprised. His face lit up, and it seemed like he wanted to jump out of his seat as he exclaimed, "Yes, that's what it is. Thank you!"

In a time of surprise, silence can be misinterpreted or misunderstood, which is all the more reason to communicate our feelings when faced with new, unexpected, or unusual information.

## *Apprehensive*

> **adj:** 1. viewing the future with anxiety or alarm;
> 2. feeling or showing suspicion about the future
>
> **The opposite of apprehensive is certain.**

Apprehension comes when you are anticipating the worst. You might feel apprehensive about going on a blind date. (Blind dates are dreadful!) It might be how you feel about going to the DMV on your lunch break—when everyone else in town will be there in line ahead of you. (Going to the DMV *anytime* is dreadful!) Apprehensive of what's ahead of you, you dread the unknown.

## Anxious

> **adj:** characterized by extreme uneasiness of mind or brooding fear about some contingency
>
> **The opposite of anxious is content.**

Anxious is one of the most commonly expressed fear emotions. In today's culture, anxiety is accepted, which makes it easier to talk about than other types of fear—and easier to dismiss as fear. No matter how accepted this term is, it is important to remember that *anxious* is a feeling of fear.

Note that anxious overlaps with dread and with excited. It's easy enough to see how feeling anxious about something perceived as negative can lead to dread. The overlap of anxious and excited means that these emotions go hand-in-hand. Sometimes we use the word anxious to express excitement—or say we are excited when we are actually anxious. Occasionally, we experience both feelings at the same time, like when you get your first interview for a job after college. You are excited. *Yaaaaaaayyyyy!* Then, the sudden feeling of anxiety washes over you. This is your only job interview. What if you blow it? Getting a real job signifies a step into adulthood. If it doesn't work out, you might have to live with your less-than-inspirational roommates . . . *forever.* Your excitement is real, but so is the anxious fear you feel.

**Example:** When I was a young boy, I anxiously awaited Christmas morning. Was I afraid of Christmas morning? Of course not. I was excited! But . . . I also felt some fear. I feared that rather than opening packages filled with cool toys, I would find a pair of pants, a belt, and two calendars under the tree.

The Tier-Three expressions of anxious are overwhelmed and worried.

## *Overwhelmed*

**adj:** completely overcome or overpowered by thought or feeling

**The opposite of overwhelmed is relaxed.**

The result of too much anxiety, overwhelmed is the feeling of being emotionally unable to handle your circumstances or tasks. The line between overwhelmed and worried is different for everyone, but when you hit the tipping point of feeling overwhelmed, you may feel stuck, indecisive, or shift into an anger reaction of detachment to avoid having to deal with more worry.

The mental image I immediately go to is the act of drowning. Especially when learning to swim, when the water comes "over" your head, it can send you into a panic. Being overwhelmed by emotion is not that different and can be difficult, frightening, and burdensome, but it can also lead to anger and defensiveness. The difficulty of remaining calm when in deep water and not being able to swim is nearly impossible, and so is following someone's advice to "calm down" when feeling overwhelmed. The goal is to be able to focus on what is overwhelming and ask for help by sharing what you are feeling.

## *Worried*

**adj:** 1. mentally troubled or concerned;
2. feeling or showing concern or anxiety about what is happening or might happen

**The opposite of worried is satisfied.**

Worry is a basic level of anxiety and expresses a fear that all people feel at one time or another. Some people call worry *stress*. Worry comes in different degrees and can be about things within your direct control or things that are completely beyond your control. This form of anxiety is the opposite of the feeling *satisfied*. When we are worried, we are definitely not feeling satisfied with how things are or the way they have gone.

# GET EMOTIONAL

Fear is your friend. Fear only distracts you if you try to ignore it, so lean into your fear. When you acknowledge fear, it helps you understand what needs to be conquered. Whether you are conquering something internal or having to conquer a behavior, such as public speaking or jumping out of an airplane, fear tells you an accomplishment is around the corner.

Think back on the last five to twenty years. List five achievements or goals you've conquered. Depending on where you are in your life journey, they might include graduating from college, having a baby, or maybe even moving to another state or country. Now, beside each accomplishment, list the fear you felt before or during each of these events. Use the Tier-Two and Tier-Three feeling words to guide you. Do you notice that fear precedes or co-existed with the goals you are most proud of achieving?

Can you do big things without feeling fearful. Sure. I graduated from college with a bachelor's at twenty-one, but this is not on my list of my "most proud of" accomplishments because I was not afraid of going to college. My doctorate, on the other hand, is on that list of accomplishments because I was scared of not getting accepted, worried about failing when classes got difficult, and fearful that I wouldn't get a job right away and be left with an exorbitant amount of student debt!

## Going Deeper

- How did you handle these specific fears? Did it work?

- Who in your life was affected by your reaction to these fears, and how did it affect them?

- After reading this chapter, how would you manage these fears differently?

- Currently, which Tier-Two emotions are the most difficult for you to acknowledge? What about the Tier-Three emotions?

# Fear
## Captured in a Quote

"The only thing we have to fear is fear itself."
—Franklin D. Roosevelt

"My fear is my 'substance' and probably the best part of me."
—Franz Kafka

"Courage is resistance to fear, mastery of fear, not absence of fear."
—Mark Twain

"Ignorance is the parent of fear."
—Herman Melville

"Do not worry about your difficulties in mathematics. I can assure you mine are still greater."
—Albert Einstein

"Fear is the path to the Dark Side."
—Yoda, *The Empire Strikes Back*

# Joy

> Find out where joy resides and give
> it a voice far beyond singing.
> For to miss the joy is to miss all.
> —*Robert Louis Stevenson*

**BELLA STRUGGLED WITH ANXIETY DAILY.** Her fears ranged from her car breaking down to losing her job to her phone crashing and leaving her without a way to call for help. Other people may share these worries, but for Bella, they were debilitating. Her anxiety grew for years, and by the time she sought counseling, she was experiencing extreme panic attacks.

I (Susan) had been seeing Bella for three years when I introduced a cognitive intervention, a therapy approach of reflecting on and reframing beliefs and thoughts. (I know this is a book about feeling rather than thinking, but hear me out.) Bella thrived with this approach because it empowered her to shift her feelings by changing the focus of her thoughts. For example, I once asked her if she had kept track of how many times her phone had *not* crashed and left her stranded. She paused before answering and said, "Well, I haven't really thought of my phone working well. I only think of it letting me down."

She began to realize that her debilitating worries focused on things that had either never happened to her or happened very rarely. Her phone worked normally, her car always started, and she had a great job. Focusing on and working to find the joyful moments each day (when things worked as they should) decreased the anxiety and sadness she felt.

Joy is often present—and ignored. In most people's lives, in fact, joy exists as much as fear, sadness, or anger. The human brain simply doesn't notice joy as readily as it does other emotions because it is too busy trying to stop or avoid the feelings on the left side of the Feeling Grid. As a result, we spend our mental energy thinking about what we don't want rather than what we do want or already have. This focus makes us so attuned to sadness, fear, and anger that, if we don't pay attention, we may fail to notice opportunities for joy.

Moving to the right side of the Feeling Grid is the goal of therapy. We devoted the first several chapters of this book to equipping you to figure out how you really feel. Identifying where you are on the Feeling Grid shows you the path to the emotions you *want* to feel, like joy, empowerment, or peace. Getting there requires intentionality. Sure, you may occasionally stumble upon moments of joy, but when you *look* for it, you may be surprised to see it everywhere.

We have to train ourselves to seek joy, especially when we are feeling sad, mad, or scared. Joy, however, often evolves out of sadness. It is our sadness that alerts us of our need for the emotions in the Joy portion of the Feeling Grid. One of the major differences in these contrasting basic emotions is that, while sadness can show up in your life uninvited, joy doesn't show up without an invitation. Joy must be invited. When you feel sadness, only you can transform it into joy. Shifting from sadness into joy requires two key things:

1. We must understand what joy is.
2. We must seek joy.

## WHAT IS JOY?

Merriam-Webster defines joy as "the emotion evoked by well-being, success, or good fortune or by the prospect of possessing what one desires." Joy is hope. It can also be excitement in the moment or happiness for the future.

Although, unlike happiness or excitement, joy runs deep—it comes from within. You experience joy on a spiritual level, not just a surface level. It looks different for everyone, and the way it shows up in your life may change depending on your circumstances. For some people, joy is what it feels like to be without sadness, loneliness, or despair. Others are more joyful when they actively feel excited or grateful.

What you might be picking up on is that you are the one who defines your joy, so you must spend time with yourself to know what joy looks like on you. In fact, getting to know yourself brings a feeling of joyfulness.

### You Must Seek Joy

Let's go back to the definition of joy: "the emotion evoked by well-being, success, or good fortune or by the prospect of possessing what one desires." Success is *sought*, and desires are possessed *by prospecting*. This definition does not depict someone sitting around waiting for something good to happen. Action is involved! Your job is to seek. Jesus says it in the New Testament, Matthew 7:7 (ESV): "Ask, and it will be given to you; seek, and you will find; knock, and it will be opened to you."

Seek, and you will find. Note that seeking joy is different from the message of the popular mantra of *choose joy!* While you can choose *not* to have joy, regardless of what the meme, sticker, or T-shirt implies, you cannot "choose joy" and expect it to appear magically. In the same way that synaptic connections form in the brain through repeated thoughts and actions, you grow joy in your life through the practice of seeking it.

This practice of seeking intentionally allows joy to take root within you. As you learn to recognize joy, those roots grow and help you connect more naturally to joy in and around you.

One of Bryan's favorite movies is *Rudy*. It's one of those movies that gives him goosebumps every time he talks about it. This feel-good movie from the 1990s is based on a true story of a young man named Rudy Ruettiger who grew up outside of Chicago, surrounded by lifetime Catholic diehard Notre Dame fans. Rudy believed his only path to attaining joy was to be part of the Notre Dame football team. He is devastated when he doesn't make the roster for the final home game of the season. His sadness quickly turns into anger, and he storms out of the locker room and decides to quit the team. He feels defeated, having worked for two years to get on the field wearing the Notre Dame uniform. When you watch the movie, you are sitting right there with him in his hopelessness. Later, Rudy's former boss, who understood how hard he had worked to make the team, shows up to talk to Rudy. You expect him to commiserate with Rudy, but he doesn't. Instead, he points out everything Rudy had accomplished and what he was missing:

> You're five-foot nothin', 100 and nothin', and you have barely a speck of athletic ability. And you hung in there with the best college football players in the land for two years. And you're gonna walk outta here with a degree from the University of Notre Dame. In this life, you don't have to prove nothin' to nobody but yourself. And after what you've gone through, if you haven't done that by now, it ain't gonna never happen. Now go on back.[11]

When his anger and fear overshadowed his joy, Rudy focused only on what was not happening for him. Was he still sad after his boss's pep talk? Yes. But the sadness fades as Rudy becomes aware of all the moments he has missed out on celebrating. As he starts to seek joy, he realizes it is rooted in the goals he has already attained and the person he has become because of it. He had to seek out the joy in his life to experience it.

So what does joy look like to you? Maybe you do not know where to look or what to look for. That's okay. This is something that takes practice. Remember, you have not been in training to seek joy. You have probably been in training to protect yourself with anger. After all, your amygdala, the small, almond-shaped area of your brain that processes emotion, is constantly on the lookout for threats. One of its primary jobs is to alert you of fear and help you survive from one day to the next. Seeking joy against all odds takes practice!

## HOW TO SEEK JOY

The Feeling Grid helps you identify not only what you feel but also what you want to feel. If you don't have the words to express how you currently feel, you can start on the right and identify what you want to feel. Alternatively, if you are starting on the left side of the grid, you can look to the right side of the grid to know what is missing. Knowing what you need can allow you to shift out of feelings of sadness, anger, or fear.

The opposite emotion of joy is sad. Sadness is present when you are experiencing feelings of apathy, hurt, loneliness, despair, guilt, or shame. If you identify that you are feeling lonely, you can look across the Feeling Grid to see that the underlying need is to feel whole. Seeking joy, then, would include asking: *What makes me feel whole?* If you recognize that the sadness you feel is shame, you can look to the right to see that shame comes from a lack of hope. From there, you can ask: *What would help me feel hopeful?*

Joy presents as six different feelings. Are there more feelings that describe Joy? Probably, but the goal is to give you a place to start. Excited, Grateful, Whole, Happy, Free, and Hopeful are all feelings that fall under Joy. Some feelings of Joy are more difficult to acquire than others. Gratitude, hope, and whole, for example, seem toughest for most of our clients, which is understandable. We don't walk around looking for things to make us whole or build hope. Gratitude may sound like a simple practice if we're just talking about saying thank you. Internalizing gratitude and making it part of your daily experience is more difficult. But the deep effect that living in gratitude can have, such as feeling whole or hopeful, is worth the effort.

The emotions that are more easily acquired—happy, excited, and free—can be fleeting. That doesn't mean happiness or excitement are not important and helpful; it simply means they fade over time. As long as you know they are fleeting, they are safe to enjoy.

## Finding Joy in Unexpected Places

Remember Bella from the chapter opening? Early in her therapeutic journey, she faced big decisions and changes, including moving into her own place and coming to terms with the reality of her impending divorce. She felt trapped by the choices she had to make. She liked living near her family, but she also dreamed of moving to a new town. She was a planner, and the devastation of the divorce left a gaping hole in her vision of the future. You might think that finding joy in such a time of turmoil and upheaval would be impossible. But it was there. Even in the midst of uncertainty and heartbreak, Bella found a spark of joy.

During one of our therapy sessions, I asked Bella what it felt like to realize that, although the divorce was in the works, she was financially stable and could afford to live on her own and take care of herself and her two children.

She said, "You know, I'm sad, and I am scared of what is coming. But I thought I was going to feel like a failure as I began the divorce process. As I move forward, though, I feel like there is hope, and I don't know why."

I smiled. I handed Bella the Feeling Grid (my handy framed copy) and asked her to find the feeling of shame. Shame is the opposite of hope. Bella had struggled with feeling ashamed of filing for divorce. The more we face what we feel ashamed of, the less power shame has over us and the more hopeful—*joy*—we begin to feel. Bryan and I believe that intentionally seeking the emotions you desire is what allows them to take root in your life. The more you nurture wanted or needed emotions, the deeper and wider their roots grow—which makes feelings, like joy, more accessible. Just like the dendrites in the brain.

Dendrites aren't static due to the phenomenon of plasticity. Plasticity is the continual growth of dendrites into later adulthood, way past the developmental phases in early childhood. Scientists used to believe that the brain stopped growing brain cells (and dendrites) once humans passed through specific developmental milestones early in life. The growth happens if stimulated, so I suppose we could say emotions have plasticity if stimulated and practiced.

You won't always know what joy looks like until you seek it, which means that looking for it can feel like a leap of faith. It requires stepping out, not knowing if the search will be worth your effort. It means letting go of sadness, which can seem difficult because of the comfort it brings you. But the odds are in your favor. Choosing to stay sad will most likely lead to feelings of anger—the opposite direction of joy.

Recognize Sad. Seek Joy.

*You won't always know what joy looks like until you seek it, which means that looking for it can feel like a leap of faith.*

## BIRTHDAY CAKE

Clients are always surprised when I ask how comfortable they are with being uncomfortable. They often respond with, "What is the point of uncomfortable?"

In your search for joy, *uncomfortable happens*. This is why I spend time helping my clients become comfortable with being uncomfortable. Spending time getting to know yourself and seeking joy can be uncomfortable. Most people retreat from the uncomfortable and search for a quick fix. We see opportunities for happiness and latch on—hoping that happiness is enough. The problem is that quick fixes, like happiness and excitement, wear off. When the happy moment passes, we're back to feeling sad. While happiness and excitement are parts of joy, each is fleeting and should only be used for the short moment that they last.

Happiness is a feeling within the emotion of joy, so why am I telling you not to seek it? Because happiness can be like the sirens in the novel *The Odyssey*. The sirens lured sailors with their beautiful songs, deceitfully causing shipwrecks. A constant pursuit of the fleeting feeling of happiness causes similar damage in our lives by distracting us from things that are more important and more deeply felt. Relying on happiness to stick around can steal one's identity.

Happiness is a fine feeling, and it is just as present in our world as sadness or fear. So learn how to experience happiness. Notice it. You can even create opportunities for it. But allow happiness to be what it is: a shallow-rooted, fun feeling that, like birthday cake, belongs to a moment in time.

There's nothing wrong with birthday cake, right? When I was a kid, I always felt awkward at birthday parties. I didn't like going and would try to avoid them, but my mom thought it was rude not to go if I was invited. The saving grace of a birthday party (and the leverage my mom used) was the promise of birthday cake. Off I went, present in hand, anticipating some amazing birthday cake. As soon as the birthday cake was gone, so was any reason for being at the birthday party. I'd go from happy to excruciatingly bored. I don't even want to talk about what happened when there was no birthday cake.

Happiness can be a wonderful feeling, but like birthday cake, it is short-lived—and doesn't stick around. Happiness is too often the ultimate goal in life. Self-help books push happiness as the answer to all your problems. We hear from clients every day who are searching for this fleeting emotion:

- I just want to be happy.
- If only my children were happy, then I would know I was a good parent.
- When XYZ happens, then I'll be happy.
- I was happier when . . .

The pursuit of happiness is exhausting, and maintaining a feeling of happiness is not realistic. We are not opposed to feeling happy or hoping for someone's happiness, but our hope is that you will focus on seeking out the longer-lasting and stable emotion of joy.

## State-based vs. Trait-based Emotions

Happiness is an example of a state-based emotion. Like a good movie or a fun conversation over coffee with a friend, it is there one minute, gone the next. Happiness, a temporary condition of mind or temperament, is often based on external circumstances. Going to a carnival, getting a puppy, or winning the lottery can bring you happiness—until you run out of tickets, the puppy makes a mess on your new rug, or, like 70 percent of lottery winners, you go bankrupt.[12]

True joy can become a trait-based emotion—an inherent quality of your personal character. As you practice seeking joy, all the emotions found in the Joy portion of the Feeling Grid become more readily available, even when life gets really uncomfortable. After a break-up, for example, trait-based joy will help you focus on the positive relationships you have in your life. If you get a speeding ticket the day after you get paid, you might automatically find comfort in the realization that you can afford to pay the ticket in a timely manner. You may still be sad that you can't buy that really cool shirt you wanted, but you will recognize the joy of being able to pay the ticket.

When I attended the birthday parties I dreaded as a kid, I was not seeking joy; I was merely waiting for happy to show up in the form of icing and cake. Had I opened myself to playing with the other children and not merely focused on the one thing I knew that would make me happy, I might have discovered more about myself. In the process, I would have been learning how to seek joy in the moment.

Enjoy the birthday cake when the opportunity arises. Just don't try to live on cake and icing alone.

## BECOMING FLUENT

Outside of writing and seeing clients in our practice, I (Susan) teach psychological statistics to graduates and undergraduates. I love teaching statistics. When I realized I wanted to teach statistics, I knew I had to master the ability to explain classical test theory and its formulas under pressure without thinking. So for the final three years of my graduate work, I practiced by offering free tutoring. (It's how I met my husband too.) The zero-dollar price tag let me off the perfection hook with an unspoken disclaimer: *I might not know the answer or be very good at this at the moment.* Then one day, I realized I could see the explanation in my head before attempting to say it aloud. That's when I knew I was becoming proficient enough to label my statistics skills as fluent.

This is what Bryan and I are talking about when we state that talking emotions takes practice. Practice is how you become fluent in the language of emotion. Even though everyone is born with emotion, the fluency with which you identify and express emotion is developed over time with practice. When a new client tells me she wants to feel more confident and unashamed around her mom, that's practice. She's identifying what she wants. Becoming fluent in her emotions will mean that she learns to recognize that she is angry and sad because she feels judged by her mom—emotions she hasn't acknowledged yet.

Can you become fluent in your emotions and know how you feel *in the moment*? Yes, but you have to begin working toward understanding your emotion instead of working against it. You need to lean into your sadness to be able to seek joy.

Our brains are wired to know when fear exists; the amygdala makes sure of that. Our brains don't, however, naturally seek out joy, which makes sense. In the theory of survival, safety is the primary goal. This could be why feelings on the left side of the Feeling Grid seem more natural.

*In the theory of survival, safety is the primary goal. This could be why feelings on the left side of the Feeling Grid seem more natural.*

What if seeking joy could feel more natural? It can if you practice. In fact, with enough repetition, seeking joy becomes organic and natural. When that happens, instead of living in sadness or investing all your time in distractions to avoid what you don't want to feel, you realize you are accepting the sadness. And sadness tells you where you are—and what you need. This is why we encourage clients to learn to become comfortable feeling uncomfortable. If you allow yourself to feel (rather than ignore or avoid) sadness, you will begin to understand what you're feeling and will be empowered to use that awareness to seek joy. Leaning into the uncomfortableness will pay off if you allow it, as long as you are practicing with your emotion.

One way to increase your joy fluency is to practice the terminology. It's likely that the words on the right side of the Feeling Grid are not all that natural for you. What we noticed while creating the Feeling Grid was that some of the words in the Joy Box are not universally used. Take a few minutes right now to think of six joyful adjectives that you use on a daily basis *and* that are familiar to the people in your life. Go ahead: Say excited, grateful, whole, happy, free, and hope aloud. Do they roll off the tongue naturally? Have you used any of those words in conversation in the past week?

We don't use joyful terminology as naturally as we do all the feelings on the left side of the grid. Not using words that relate to feelings of joy on a normal basis makes them unfamiliar, which can make the feelings more difficult to seek or connect with. Using these joyful terms will help create fluency—for you and the people in your life—because sometimes, seeking joy is simply sharing our experiences.

## SPREAD THE JOY

Susan and I ride to and from work together. One day, on the way home from work, Susan said, "Okay, I don't think I should be a counselor anymore. I wasn't very good at listening today. I wanted to hurry things along and fix a few people, tell a few other people they were making big mistakes, but mostly, I thought maybe I should quit to not hurt them in any way with my bad counseling." It wasn't the first or last time she offered this post-work summary, although 95 percent of the time, she talked about loving her job.

I began our commute in a completely different headspace, dabbling with the idea that I could be the best psychologist ever! If there was a Golden Cardigan Sweater Trophy, I would have won it in a landslide! I was on fire that day, and I was excited to tell her all about it. But then I was perplexed as she expressed her sadness: *Should I share my joy, or would talking about it make her feel worse?* I took a chance and decided to share what I was feeling after having such a great day. I told her about the insights gained by clients and how my typical overuse of metaphors came in handy.

Silence.

The car was quiet except for the sound of the Sirius XM Yacht Rock channel playing in the background. I worried that I might have increased Susan's sadness by pointing out that I didn't have a bad day. Had I rubbed her sadness in her face?

Those worries swirled in my mind until she smiled and asked me a question about one of my clients that allowed me to continue sharing my kick-butt-psychologist day. Later, I asked her what she was feeling when I began talking about my "very most excellent day." She said I had caught her off guard at first, but then she began feeling joy for me and eventually moved out of her own sadness. She also said that when she offered some ideas about my interactions with clients, she began to feel less unworthy or incapable.

One crucial element that helped Susan move from sad toward joy is that her joy is trait-based. She is intentional about seeking joy, which allows her to not get consumed by sadness or allow anger to get in the way with irritation or jealousy. Her sharing her sadness and admitting to some counseling moments that went badly was a form of her working through her sadness. She was seeking joy and was able to hear it in my experiences of the day.

Notice, too, that she felt multiple emotions at the same time—both sadness and joy. My good day didn't make Susan's joy complete, but sharing the joy from my day helped her move toward joy. So yes, sometimes we seek joy simply by sharing our experiences, but sometimes, by sharing our experiences, we empower others to find joy.

## CONCLUSION

It would seem that the biggest problem that people have with joy is one of two expectations:

1. Joy should last a long time.

2. Joy will never last a long time.

The belief that joy should be forever only highlights our disappointment when we cannot maintain our joy. It is a surface level of living when we think that all things are joyous and nothing can bring us down. This is a daydream—or maybe a nightmare. There is constant pressure to always be "on" and never let anyone down. Nobody can maintain this. Joy may be present, but reality is that we all feel sadness as well. The good news is that sadness and joy work together.

The expectation that joy can never last very long comes from neglecting to recognize joy when it is present. This is the opposite direction of seeking joy because now you are looking for ways to be sad. The other shoe may drop, but what does another shoe have to do with your joy in the moment? You could pause your joy and wait, then prove yourself to be right. Sadness came back. Or you could relish your joy for that moment.

All these experiences will be a challenge at first. The fact that this is a challenge does not make you incapable or inferior. You just have to put this into practice. You might surprise yourself with how quickly you can move away from sadness as you seek joy. You also might be relieved that when sadness returns, as it undoubtedly will, the sadness will not be as demoralizing as it has been in the past.

# JOY EMOTIONS

| TIER 3 | TIER 2 | |
|---|---|---|
| Enthusiastic / Passionate | **Excited** | **JOYFUL** |
| Fortunate / Appreciated | **Grateful** | |
| Cherished / Noticed | **Whole** | |
| Pleased / Elated | **Happy** | |
| Liberated / Delighted | **Free** | |
| Proud / Honored | **Hope** | |

## Excited

**adj:** having, showing, or characterized by a heightened state of energy, enthusiasm, eagerness, etc.

**The opposite of excited is apathetic.**

What you get excited about is unique to you, but it is certainly about joy. You may be excited about an upcoming event or holiday, the change of seasons, or a day off. When you are excited about something, you may notice the overlap that occurs vertically on the Feeling Grid. Excitement sits right above grateful and below anxious. You might experience that overlap of emotions after getting a promotion at work—excitement about your new role, grateful for the opportunity, and worried about making a mistake. Excitement is a fun feeling that, if based on a temporary circumstance, can quickly fade. The Tier-Three emotions associated with excited, enthusiastic, and passionate are similar, but each has a unique nuance.

## *Enthusiastic*

**adj:** strong excitement of feeling: ARDOR

**The opposite of enthusiastic is indifferent.**

Enthusiastic is a form of excitement derived from the Greek word *enthousiasmós*, which means "to be inspired." The inspiration that influences an enthusiastic feeling gives it a distinction that separates it from passionate. More importantly, indifference is not a quality of the inspired.

## *Passionate*

**adj:** capable of, affected by, or expressing intense feeling

**The opposite of passionate is numb.**

The difference between enthusiastic and passionate is the intensity and longevity of the emotion. Whereas enthusiasm for an interest may pass quickly, passion, when it is internally based, can be enduring. Sometimes, the best way to understand the meaning of a word on the Feeling Grid is to look at its opposites. In this case, *numb*. Numb expresses an absence of care that has built up over time; passion expresses extreme care and might be the thing that pushes us to start a business, join a cause, or run for political office in hopes of bringing about change for a community we care about. Our passions exist beyond a moment.

## Grateful

**adj:** 1. appreciative of benefits received;
2. affording pleasure: PLEASING

**The opposite of grateful is hurt.**

Grateful is the emotion that is the opposite of hurt. When we are hurting, we are not grateful. When our hurt ends, we are grateful. This is how we came to this conclusion to add grateful to the Feeling Grid. Within gratefulness, we begin to recognize our freedom from pain. You might use expressions like, "It could be worse." Such a statement acknowledges the existence of pain as well as absence of more substantial pain. What it does not acknowledge is appreciation. We must call attention to our gratitude. If we are going to seek joy, we need to use joy words. Stating that it could be worse might be accurate, but it is focusing on our pain, not seeking joy.

## *Fortunate*

**adj:** 1. bringing some good thing not foreseen as certain;
2. receiving some unexpected good

**The opposite of fortunate is disappointed.**

The emotion of disappointment can often come when an expectation is not met. We feel fortunate when we recognize the good that exists with, and particularly without, regard to expectation. If the package we were expecting to be delivered did not show, then we might feel disappointed. If the package came a day earlier than expected, we might feel fortunate.

Fortunate is another emotional expression that is not very common in our everyday speech. This word expresses gratitude, which makes it a feeling that should be shared. People tend not to share this joyful feeling, however, because doing do can seem like bragging; there is always someone who is less fortunate. I wonder if one reason we do not share this feeling is because it can create feelings of exposure, embarrassment, or the possibility of being rejected or judged.

## *Appreciated*

**adj:** 1a. to grasp the nature, worth, quality, or significance of; 1b. to value or admire highly

**The opposite of appreciated is betrayed.**

The purpose of appreciation days, whether for teachers, bosses, first responders, or secretaries, is to show appreciation for all that person does. Do you think they feel betrayed if the day isn't celebrated? Maybe, but probably not. But what if your spouse or child never showed you how much they appreciate you? Would you feel less worthy, less significant, or less admired or valued? Over time, yes. Now, imagine that the person you do not feel appreciated by is showing appreciation toward someone else. This is when betrayal enters the relationship.

Betrayal has often been the precursor to feeling unappreciated. Feeling appreciated takes action on the part of the person to realize their worth, significance, and value, as well as action on the part of the person reaping the benefits of someone.

## Whole

**adj:** 1. free of defect or impairment;
2. having all its proper parts or components: COMPLETE, UNMODIFIED;
3. constituting an undivided unit: UNBROKEN, UNCUT

**The opposite of whole is lonely.**

At first glance, *whole* doesn't sound like an emotion but a state of being. This is actually the point. When we are feeling whole, whether we are by ourselves or in the company of others, we do not feel lonely, which is the opposite emotion.

The purpose of using the word lonely generates a sense of feeling empty. The experience of feeling whole is to be in a relationship that is working, thriving, engaging, and valued.

**Example:** When our children were much younger, Susan took them with her out of town to visit her brother's family. I wasn't able to get away from work, and a colleague asked if I was lonely since my family was gone and I was by myself. My reply was, "Of course not. I still have them; they just are not here." I know Susan still cherishes me when she is out of town, and we talk throughout the time she is away. I might be alone, but I am not lonely because I still feel whole. Lonely is the wrong feeling. It might be more accurate to say that I was sad that I was not with them.

## *Cherished*

**adj:** 1. kept or cultivated with care and affection: NURTURED; 2. entertained or harbored in the mind deeply and resolutely

**The opposite of cherished is abandoned.**

When we are feeling cherished, we are not feeling abandoned. The word cherish actually came to mind when I thought of wedding vows. "Do you take this woman to have and to hold, to love and to cherish?" The idea is that marriage is a union and, ideally, creates feelings that are the opposite of both lonely and abandoned. Knowing that someone cherishes and loves you also creates feelings of wholeness (completeness).

## *Noticed*

**adj:** To treat with attention: to become aware of

**The opposite of noticed is neglected.**

With neglect, there is an omission of someone in your presence, yet to be noticed would be an end to neglect. It allows one person to not only believe that they exist but to feel less broken—whole. It is a powerful experience to be noticed by someone who has been around you. It seems like every John Hughes film from the 1980s has a character who struggles with neglect and is changed by being noticed. *Sixteen Candles, Ferris Bueller's Day Off, The Breakfast Club, Some Kind of Wonderful, Pretty in*

*Pink*, and *Weird Science*—all of them have a character that feels neglected in some way. They talk about it, and within the group of friends, they become noticed.

## Happy

**adj:** 1. favored by luck or fortune;
2. notably fitting, effective, or well-adapted;
3. enjoying or characterized by well-being;
4. glad, pleased

**The opposite of happy is despair.**

Happy says, "Everything is going my way!" It highlights an emotional experience within a moment and is something everyone can feel, yet briefly. As explained in "Birthday Cake!" (page 160), while happiness is important, it is not sustainable or internally based and should not be your primary emotion on the right side of the grid.

### *Pleased*

**v:** to give pleasure to

**The opposite of pleased is grief.**

A simple expression of happiness, pleased can be related to a sense of accomplishment, like how you feel when you take pride in a job well done. It can be a completed task, like the neat, even lines of a freshly mown lawn, the way you aced that exam, the knowledge that you've served or honored someone well, or the feeling when you know you've given someone you love the perfect gift. The opposite of pleased is grief, which we encounter as the result of loss.

## *Elated*

**adj:** Marked by high spirits: exultant

**The opposite of elated is dejected.**

Elated is on the high end of happy. Whereas pleased might be expressed as a gentle smile, hug, or pat on the back, *exultant*, expresses the feeling of rejoicing in triumph. Picture the scene when a sports announcer exclaims, "And the crowd goes wild!" When you feel elated, your face and body demonstrate your happiness to the world around you.

## Free

**adj:** 1. not costing or charging anything;
4a. relieved from or lacking something and especially something unpleasant or burdensome

**The opposite of free is guilty.**

Here's another word that doesn't *seem* like it is an emotion, but feeling free is such a liberating experience. (*Ba-dum-ba!*) Sorry, we couldn't help ourselves. Seriously, though, free is a feeling that causes great delight and moves us away from the burdening emotion of guilt. Imagine the sensation of a weight being lifted off your shoulders, having a spring in your step, and knowing the choices for your future are endless and filled with ease. That's what free feels like.

## *Liberated*

**adj:** released or freed from

**The opposite of liberated is remorseful.**

I mentioned earlier that finding the right words for the Feeling Grid, particularly this side of the grid, was quite difficult. Such was the case for the opposite of *remorseful*. Remorse is a sadness that comes from feeling sorry for our actions. When we are released or *liberated* from our guilt, the emotional freedom is undeniable. Imagine feeling guilty your whole life. The longer the guilt lasts, the more it imprisons you, inhibiting your actions, hindering your relationships, and limiting the way you view yourself—your worth or capability. Now imagine being suddenly freed from that prison. Your shackles fall to the ground, and the invisible bars that have held you captive are gone! You are *liberated*, free to enjoy life to the fullest.

## Delighted

**adj:** highly pleasing

**The opposite of delighted is miserable.**

Delighted has a similar style or connection to sadness. The opposite of delighted is miserable. Miserable is the state of great unhappiness or profound sadness based on a circumstance. Delighted is now a way to be free of that misery. The word also has the root "light," as in not heavy. To be delighted to join someone for lunch would mean that we would be free from the misery of eating alone or even not eating at all. To be honest, delighted is not a common word I hear unless I am watching the Great British Baking Show. And honestly, this is probably one of the reasons our family enjoys watching it—the number of joyful words used, with delightful being one of their favorites.

## Hope

**v:** 1. to desire with expectation of obtainment or fulfillment;
2. to expect with confidence: TRUST

**The opposite of hope is shame.**

You will notice at this point that the word *hopeless* is not on the Feeling Grid. This is true, in part, because the more specifically you can speak about your emotions of sadness, the better the chances are that someone will be able to connect with how you are feeling.

Hopelessness is a generic term that's often used when we can't find the words to express how we truly feel. It can leave people who want to comfort us with more questions than answers. Usually, our hopes are easier to clearly express. Often, it's the way we begin or end a statement: *I feel so much hope because . . .* or *Knowing XYZ gives me such a sense of hope.*

Shame, an internal feeling based on an external source, sits opposite of hope on the Feeling Grid. The contrast is vivid: Shame takes away the trust and confidence we feel in ourselves; hope restores that trust and confidence. Hope gives us light at the end of the dark tunnel. Shame just calls the tunnel a cave and says there is no way out.

## Proud

**adj:** 1. having or displaying excessive self-esteem

**The opposite of proud is worthless.**

You can feel proud of others or yourself. This word is the opposite of worthless, which is evident in the definition of "excessive self-esteem." You cannot have self-esteem, excessive or otherwise, without a sense of personal value or worth. Feeling this sense of pride can lead to hope in and for ourselves as well.

It wasn't until the most recent iteration of the Feeling Grid that we added the word proud. It's a word people are often willing to use regarding others but are hesitant to say about themselves. Consider which statement below would be easier to say aloud:

I'm so proud of my kids because of their kindness toward others.

I'm so proud of myself for stopping to help that person today.

For most people, the first statement is no problem. The second is laced with concerns about stepping over the line and being too prideful. *Pride is a sin,* we remind ourselves. *I don't want to sound too proud.*

But pride can be a good thing if you don't take it to excess. That's true of most things, isn't it? Milk is good for you. I love milk. But I still remember hearing when I was twelve that drinking a gallon of milk in an hour could kill you. Twelve-year-old Bryan's fear of death by milk sounds ridiculous to my present-day psychologist self. I don't know the exact correlation between physical well-being and too much milk, but I do know that most things taken to excess aren't good for you. Hopefully, you see my point. Pride—in yourself, your team, or your country—can give you a sense of purpose and worth and can even foster community. Just don't take it so far that it interferes with your relationships.

## *Honored*

>**v:** 1. regarded or treated with admiration and respect;
>2. to live up to or fulfill the terms of;
>3. to salute with a bow in square dancing
>
>**The opposite of honored is inferior.**

Honors and awards are not for the shamed but for those who have achieved respect. We honor those individuals as a way to feel connected with them as well.

If you know anything about square dancing (I don't), you may know it's important to "honor your partner." Ladies curtsey, and gentlemen bow in acknowledgment of their partners before they begin do-si-doing around the dance hall. All the turning and stomping while arm-in-arm seems like a workout in pressed shirts, frilly dresses, and boots, but it starts in a good place by honoring—connecting—with the person in front of you.

# GET EMOTIONAL

The goal in joy is based on seeking out your joy. Not only is seeking joy a difficult task at times, but outwardly expressing that joy brings hesitation. We can be hesitant to share our feelings of joy in fear that it might be bragging or even hurt others when their day is not as great as ours. So there is no fuel to our joy, and the flame goes out.

I have many clients who never give joy its due. They are "waiting for the other shoe to drop" or expecting it to be a brief encounter. Of course, joy is temporary, just like all the other feelings. But if we never even look at it, we will never notice it. The goal in getting deeper is to be able to share your joy at any time, regardless of the outcome. Let people know about your joy. Pick two different people to share your excitement, passion, gratitude, hopes, elation, or what you cherish. Let joy stand up.

## Going Deeper

- Did you find joy that you didn't know you had?

- How did your efforts to seek joy impact your day/week/month?

- Did your joy have an impact on others? Negatively or positively?

- Did they become more emotional?

# Joy
## Captured in a Quote

"Joy is the serious business of heaven."
—C.S. Lewis

"The pain of parting is nothing compared to the joy of meeting again."
—Charles Dickens

"The noblest pleasure is the joy of understanding."
—Leonardo DaVinci

"Joy is prayer; joy is strength; joy is love; joy is a net of love by which you can catch souls."
—Mother Teresa

"We must accept finite disappointment but never lose infinite hope."
—Martin Luther King, Jr.

"For every minute you are angry, you lose sixty seconds of happiness."
—Ralph Waldo Emerson

# Peaceful

> It isn't enough to talk about peace. One must believe in it. And it isn't enough to believe in it. One must work at it.
> —*Eleanor Roosevelt*

"ARE YOU OKAY?" Susan asked for the third time.

I was bothered by her repeated questioning. Well, that and the fact that it was the hottest day of the year, and I had chosen that day to take my family on a camping trip to Enchanted Rock, just outside of Austin, Texas. "Yes," I said, wiping the sweat off my forehead with my shirt. "Why do you keep asking?"

"I have never seen you so, I don't know . . . quiet," she replied. "It's like you have something on your mind, but you don't know how to talk about it."

I assured her nothing was wrong. Despite being extremely sticky and sweaty, I was having a great time.

Fast forward nearly five years later, Isabel and James were ten years old, and we headed out for our second family camping trip. This time, we spent four nights tent camping in the Great Smokey Mountains in

North Carolina. The weather was perfect, and I was excited to share this amazing, adventurous experience with my family.

The first morning, Susan and I were sitting outside our tent drinking disgusting campfire-heated-up coffee when she looked at me, concerned. "Are you okay?" she asked.

"Um, yes . . ." I replied. My thoughts immediately went back to our first camping trip. I hoped I wouldn't be answering the same question over and over again for the next four days.

Her mind went to the same place. "The way you're acting reminds me of the first time we went camping."

We sat quietly for a moment before she asked, "Are you sure you are not worrying about anything? Anxious about anything, like maybe a bear or something that could eat us?"

Her question made me take stock of how I felt, and I realized something surprising: I was not stressing about anything. I was without fear at the moment. When I am outdoors, I am at the most peaceful place in my soul. Some of my greatest moments and most peaceful memories, in fact, occurred when I was working toward my Eagle Scout badge, spending time with my dad outside learning to just be with nature.

Being outdoors with my family and relying only on nature and the simple, short list of amenities that an Eagle Scout needs to survive felt good—*relaxing*. In that moment, with the terrible coffee and the birds chirping, I felt completely peaceful.

Peaceful wasn't a normal state for me, and Susan noticed the difference in my demeanor. What Susan was seeing in me was something new—something she had seen me experience only once before back at Enchanted Rock: a complete lack of fear. We had both been in graduate school when we met, so camping wasn't something we had experienced together early in our relationship. That meant Susan had only ever experienced "fearful Bryan"—the version of me who was so concerned with hiding my fear so I could appear all-knowing, relaxed, and trustworthy.

Clearly, though, she saw the difference between the peaceful me and the one who only pretended to be calm, cool, and collected.

## WHERE DOES PEACE COME FROM?

Bryan isn't alone in his admission of living in a more fearful state of mind. Peace is an emotion that seems to have a short shelf-life or just beyond our grasp. We desire peace—long for it. Throughout humanity, we see the quest for inner peace, world peace, or even peace and quiet.

So where do we find it?

One place Bryan finds it is outdoors. When we went camping those first few times, Bryan's peace threw me off. I wasn't used to seeing him so completely at ease with himself, his surroundings, or even the kids and me. When he's on a non-glamping, 100 percent outdoor, no-bathroom camping trip, he feels completely at ease. He knew, of course, that he enjoyed camping and that he wanted to share those special experiences with us, but it wasn't until I started pestering him with questions that he realized exactly what he was feeling—and why. He had no idea he was experiencing the feeling of peace.

It wasn't the woods that brought Bryan peace; it was the way he experienced them. Free from self-imposed expectations, worries, and demands on his time, he felt at ease. For him, being outdoors carries special memories. It's a place where he feels content.

Bryan's introspection helped define the two important components of attaining peace:

1. Recognizing what peace feels like for you.

2. Sharing what you have recognized in yourself.

We find peace in the same place we find true joy: within ourselves. There is no formula or place you can go that guarantees you'll feel peaceful. Peace is not something you can simply describe and then go find, buy, and adopt. For instance, you can't go looking for it in the woods and expect peace to show up for you the way it does for Bryan. (If you are anything like me, the threat of bears and hitchhiking murderers ruin any chance of peace while trying to sleep in a tent.)

Peace comes from within, which means the way you attain it will be unique to you. It also means you have to be cognizant of your search for peace. So pay attention and recognize what peace feels like for you. When you experience peace, share it with others to help it grow.

Learning to relate to yourself by identifying your emotions and then sharing your feelings with others are important components of finding peace. You've seen this idea repeated throughout this book:

- When experiencing anger, understanding where the anger is coming from helps you feel less avoidant or disgusted.
- When you feel sadness, sharing your pain and suffering helps you move toward seeking joy.
- When you feel fearful, acknowledging your fear allows you to move toward feelings of peace.

When it comes to peace, acknowledging your contentment or the fact that you feel supported or even loved is what opens the door for those feelings to grow. To do that, you must spend time with yourself. Another way to state that is you need to learn to relate to yourself. Understanding yourself helps you connect with others.

## Understanding yourself helps you connect with others.

I had a client tell me one day in session that she was getting so much out of therapy this time around. She believed the difference was because she was thinking about what she talked about in session when she was not in session. For me, it was this *aha* moment as a counselor. I realized that my clients needed to spend time with themselves while they were learning to change their behaviors or grow relationships with others.

Peace is what you are working for when you go on a second date. You spend time with someone to get to know them. As you get to know someone, trust can increase. Trusting someone creates a sense of peace. My client was getting to know herself.

Bryan's revelations about himself on our camping trip made him aware of not only the peace he feels outdoors but also the fear he feels in his daily life. Noticing the lack of peace in his daily (noncamping) life allowed him to approach both peace and fear with better understanding.

## Lack of Peace = Fear

As soon as I (Bryan) recognized that I was at peace in the woods, the amount of fear I experienced in my daily life became even more clear. What I did not know was that I basically lived in fear—not just basic fear but macro fear! I literally lived in fear of living in fear. My personality and ability to connect were so overrun with fear that when my fear diminished out in the woods, my wife did not recognize me in my peaceful state. More surprisingly, *I didn't know I was at peace.* So I spent the rest of our camping trip in the Smokey Mountains talking about what it felt like to be away from all the stress and worry of our business, house, and relationships. I spent time sitting by the campfire, recognizing the lack of fear. I also thought about all the past moments when I had caved to fear. I felt closer to my family after the camping trip—not because of camping but because of sharing and spending time talking about our fears.

Did I go back to the real world a changed man? No, I still worry about almost everything. Am I working out enough to stay in shape as I get older? Will the kids ever load and unload the dishwasher correctly? Am I being a loving husband? Is Susan going to get bored with me when we get old? Will I survive the next year as the kids prepare for college?

How many more seasons can I remain hopeful that Texas Tech football could win a championship?

My fears remained, but how I worked with my fears changed. I talked about my fears. I also began to recognize some peaceful moments and talked about those too. I still share these moments with my family, my clients, and sometimes my dog, Boomer. What I think was the most amazing and interesting part of this journey into peace is that I did not know I was at peace.

Don't you think you would notice if you were not fearful anymore? Would you realize you were experiencing peace? I would have said yes before those family camping trips, but now I don't believe so. What I do know is that when fear diminishes, peace presents itself. It's my job to recognize it.

## PEACE = LACK OF FEAR

Peace presents itself in the absence of fear. Why does the elimination of fear open the door for peace? Let's go back to the dictionary and define peace.

### Peace

> **n:** 1. A state of tranquility or quiet
> 2. Freedom from disquieting or oppressive thoughts or emotions
> 3. Harmony in personal relations

The definition states that the feeling of peace exists because there is a lack of oppressive thoughts or emotions. Lack of *oppressive thoughts or emotions* is stating the less fear you have, the more likely you are to experience peace. By definition, peace equals a lack of fear. Also, by definition, acknowledging your fear is the key to attaining peace. Whether you choose to accept that peace is another story.

If the way to peace is through acknowledging fear, you need to identify what kind of fear you are feeling. You also need to know what your fear is rooted in. If you do not devote time to understanding yourself and what your fears are or where they come from, you might have trouble knowing what type of peace you are missing.

The Feeling Grid offers different feelings of peace. If you know that you are experiencing peace, use the grid to clarify the kind of peace you are experiencing. If you are not feeling peace because fear is the overarching feeling, use the Feeling Grid to narrow down which fear you are experiencing. Once you know what fear you are experiencing, you can use that to guide the feeling of peace you might need to work toward.

Working for peace is hard; there is no other way to describe it. Making yourself acknowledge your fears to understand them more is even harder. If you begin with fear (as most of us do), you are also learning to be *comfortable in the uncomfortable.*

## BEING COMFORTABLE IN THE UNCOMFORTABLE

Hello, my name is _____ _____, and I am a fearful person.

Admitting that fear exists in your life is the first step toward peace. If the only way to peace is to admit to fear, you gotta admit to your fears. That's not something most people like to do. Fear is seen as a weakness, even though everyone experiences fear. If you don't allow yourself to admit to feeling fear, the only place you end up is back in the Anger Box (avoidant, defensive, mad, selfish, hateful, or disgusted).

After acknowledging that you are experiencing fear, the next step is to lean into your fear and get to know it. Doing that successfully requires that you learn how to become comfortable with being uncomfortable.

One of my clients dealing with panic attacks described the experiences as debilitating. When she wasn't having them, she was anticipating them. She said it felt as if the panic attacks were on the other side of the door, and she never knew when one would push in the door and crush her.

"Have you ever thought about opening the door to allow them in?" I asked.

She responded with a gasp and an appalled expression, then shook her head.

Thoughtfully, I shrugged and said, "The panic attack is coming in whether you open the door or not. If it doesn't meet any resistance on its way, physics tells me it's going to be less powerful on entry."

We worked for the next couple of weeks on her allowing, even expecting, panic attacks. They came, but their intensity decreased tremendously. The next step in therapy was to assume an underlying anxiety in her day and where she should invite that to be. By spending time with her fear (anxiety, sense of overwhelm, and worry), she began to understand it, which allowed her to connect through other emotions, including peace.

Without connecting to your fears, you cannot work toward peace. Spend time learning about where your fears are rooted. Sometimes, simply saying your fears aloud lessens them and creates a sense of peace. Don't underestimate the power of simply allowing yourself to explore your fear. Hang out in there, notice the wallpaper and the temperature of the room, and get a feel for it. Notice, too, how others fit into your fear.

If you are experiencing fear without admitting to it or working to understand it, then you are most likely presenting with anger. Anger creates a disconnect in relationships. It leaves no room for peace. The more you recognize and understand your fear, the better able you are to shift out of anger, which makes you more approachable. From there, sharing how you feel will also allow you to connect with others.

If you are walking on a trail and you come across a rattlesnake, wouldn't you agree that surprise, anxiety, and apprehension might be good descriptors of how you would feel? The question is, would you acknowledge those feelings in the moment? Let's look at what choosing not to admit to fear might look like.

You could yell at the snake, criticizing it for being in your way: "Stupid snake! You are dangerous. You aren't supposed to be on my trail!"

**Is that response helpful?** No. Anger doesn't improve the situation. If anything, the snake is coiling to strike.

Alternatively, you could try to ignore or avoid the fear of the snake biting you by looking away, pretending it isn't there, and saying, "I just don't have time to think about this snake."

**Is that response helpful?** No. It sounds ridiculous! Avoiding fear (an anger reaction) doesn't improve the situation either. Continuing on your path, pretending the snake isn't there, is a recipe for disaster.

This illustration may sound silly, but it's actually no different from how we use anger in our relationships with others and ourselves. Fear is an important emotion when standing in front of a snake. It's a red flag to stop and assess the situation. When you choose to acknowledge the fear, you can find a peaceful solution. You could turn around and slowly go the other way, which allows relief, or a sense of peace. You could try to go around the snake—again, the possibility of a peaceful escape from danger. You could look for a stick that you could use to coax the snake to move off the path. This third option seems harder, but a long stick (a *very long* stick) might be useful in moving the snake off the path so you can pass with a sense of relief and peace.

> *When you choose to acknowledge the fear, you can find a peaceful solution.*

Let's say you choose this third option as your plan. How would you feel knowing you had a long stick and a safe plan of escape? Would you feel only peace, or might you feel fear and peace at the same time? In this scenario, probably both, right? At least until the snake has moved off into the woods and you are safely down the trail.

Peace and fear have an inverse relationship. As one gets strong, the other weakens. The two emotions are not mutually exclusive. Both fear and peace can be present at the same time—but only if fear is not being avoided or ignored. Avoiding or ignoring what you are afraid of will end up with you wrestling with a rattlesnake. The point is that you can experience peace while still experiencing fear. The goal is to continue to acknowledge your fears and to accept peace as it comes. It's okay if the path to peace is uncomfortable.

## LOVING SPIDERS AND SPECIFICITY

After looking at the Feeling Grid, one of Bryan's clients shook his head and said, "So you are telling me that if I am scared of spiders, I should just work at loving spiders? I'm not doing that, Bryan!" The opposite of scared is love on the Feeling Grid in the green boxes.

In all the years he had been using this tool with clients, no one had asked Bryan about loving spiders, which kind of surprised him since *love* is the opposite of *scared* on the Feeling Grid. It's a great question, though, because it challenges the rules of the Feeling Grid.

The emotions on the right of the Feeling Grid can tell us what we need. If we're scared, then we need love, right? Yes, but you don't need to love spiders, nor do you need love from spiders.

What this client needed—what we *all* need—was to get specific about his feelings. Bryan's client was using scared as a common vernacular when talking about his fear of spiders. His true feeling, however, was not *scared*.

*Scared* is often used as a catch-all term for fears of spiders, snakes, and other unloved critters, but if we get specific on the type of fear we're feeling, we can get to the real need.

Bryan explains: To figure out what type of fear he was feeling in the moment, I asked him to think about the spider's location in a given scenario. If the spider were to jump on my client's arm, he might feel helpless or vulnerable. In that case, the goal would be to move toward the feeling of security and safety. If the spider were on the outside of the window, the fearful feeling in the moment might lean more toward concerned. If that spider walked toward an opening in the window, concern might turn to dread the closer that spider got to my client's personal space. If he shut the window, the fear would dissipate and turn into feeling assured that the spider couldn't get in and bite him.

Did he feel fear? Certainly. Spending time with your emotions with the goal of being more specific in what you need (security versus love) is important and will improve knowledge of self. That understanding of self and improved ability to identify and express what you need will empower you to improve your relationship with yourself and with others.

## CONCLUSION

Peace. Stability. Calm. Serenity. Tranquility. Quiet. These sound like terms that come with ease and simplicity. What these words represent do not come with ease nor are they experienced with simplicity. Peace takes work. Trust is earned, Love takes time, and content is not an everyday occurrence. Peace is not attained through fighting, but it will take work.

*Peace is not attained through fighting, but it will take work.*

Working towards peace is effective, but we have to start with our fears. There is nothing wrong with fear—only the lack of acknowledging fear, which is what prevents us from experiencing the emotion of peace. Remember: fear is always present when we are on the cusp of great accomplishment. For peace to occur, we must acknowledge fear and work to understand what it is telling us.

# PEACEFUL EMOTIONS

| TIER 3 | TIER 2 | |
|---|---|---|
| Nurtured / Reinforced | Supported | P E A C E F U L |
| Significant / Acknowledged | Accepted | |
| Encouraged / Protected | Loved | |
| Safe / Trusted | Secure | |
| Relieved / Certain | Assured | |
| Relaxed / Satisfied | Content | |

## Supported

**v:** 1. to endure bravely or quietly;
2. to promote the interests or cause of;
3. to pay the costs of;
4. to hold up or serve as a foundation or prop for;
5. to keep from fainting, yielding, or losing courage: COMFORT;
6. to keep (something) going

**The opposite of supported is concerned.**

Clients frequently use the term *supported* in session, but they do so in the negative, as in: "I don't feel supported." When people are not feeling supported, they feel concerned—concerned that they are at risk, concerned that they might be abandoned, concerned that no one cares, concerned that they don't have what it takes, concerned about _____ (fill in the blank). When people are able to identify their concern, they are better equipped to connect with others who can provide the support they so desperately desire.

Consider how peace relates to supported. Imagine crossing a questionably built bridge that spans high over a raging river. Looking at the corroded metal, you might be fearful or, more specifically, concerned about its integrity. You might even think, *If there were only some more support to this structure, I would feel more peace about using it.*

Feeling supported gives us a sense of peace.

## Nurtured

> **v:** 1. supplied with nourishment;
> 2. educate;
> 3. to further the development of: FOSTER

**The opposite of nurtured is confused.**

When we reflect on moments of confusion in our past, some of the most compelling have either been in classrooms or in close personal relationships. Nurturing eliminates that confusion. If a teacher nurtures a student through the material, the learner feels supported and less confused. The same holds true for relationships. When we nurture one another with clarifying information about, say, our feelings or what the plan is for Saturday night or who is taking the kids to school, we eliminate ambiguity and remove confusion, which promotes peace.

## *Reinforced*

**v:** to strengthen by additional assistance, material, or support: make stronger or more pronounced

**The opposite of reinforced is embarrassed.**

When military leaders call for reinforcements, they are ensuring support is provided to the troops on the ground. Without that support, the battle might be lost. When we feel embarrassed, what we are seeking is the kind of support that reinforces our courage and confidence. That reinforcement can come in the form of someone standing beside us or with a sense of personal conviction that affirms us and allows us to let go of fear, concern, or rejection.

## Accepted

**adj:** regarded favorably: given approval, acceptance

**The opposite of accepted is rejected.**

Being accepted is a peaceful feeling that provides a sense of belonging, even importance, in a relationship. Whether the acceptance comes from colleagues, close friends, family members, or strangers on the internet, it fills a need and eases the fear that comes from feeling rejected. This is why acceptance is found in peace. There is nothing more peaceful than walking into a place where you always feel accepted. "Norm!"

## *Significant*

**adj:** 1. having meaning;
2a. having or likely to have influence or effect: IMPORTANT;
2b. probably caused by something other than mere chance

**The opposite of significant is insignificant.**

Significant highlights a high degree of acceptance in relationships. We call our mates our *significant* others because they are important to us.

Your spouse is significant because his or her life, actions, and words influence your own. It's likely that you can identify people who are significant to you, people's whose lives affect yours.

Bryan and I worked the after-hours shifts for the community's crisis and prevention center. When I was called out to meet with someone in crisis, my job was to assess their suicidal ideation. If the person was suicidal, I knew they needed something in their immediate world to grasp onto to fight the heavy despair they were feeling. Part of my job was to help them identify something or someone significant in their life. It was telling when it was difficult to find that aspect or person of significance. The feeling of significance or *insignificance* can profoundly affect our hearts and souls. When you lack significance, you lack meaning and become insignificant to the world.

Interestingly enough, the two most unique significant relationships identified by clients in crisis thus far have been a PlayStation 5 and a pet cat. My personal service announcement: Be there for your loved ones.

## *Acknowledged*

**adj:** generally recognized, accepted, or admitted

**The opposite of acknowledged is inadequate.**

Acknowledgment highlights acceptance to a lesser degree than significance and can come in a variety of forms: A stranger on the street may acknowledge you with a smile or quick nod. Your boss may say a few words of praise to acknowledge your work on a project. The teacher calls your name on the class roster while taking attendance, and you say, "Here," acknowledging you are where you're supposed to be.

**A quick story**: By the spring semester of freshmen year in college, I (Bryan) felt pretty confident about where I was and who I was. When I came to my history lab, the teaching assistant (TA) noticed the bold letters on my green high school sweatshirt: JESUIT. It turned out that the TA had attended the same high school. We bantered for a few minutes in class about the school and a few teachers we both knew. I felt acknowledged when he noticed me and had a peaceful sense that came from knowing I belonged there. Then he took attendance, and my name was not on the roster. The quick twinge of rejection I felt at being overlooked quickly vanished when the TA told me he would get it sorted out. It felt good to know that my being there mattered to him. I didn't have the words or awareness to describe it back then, but what I felt was a feeling of significance. Too bad it didn't last.

As the lab progressed, I realized I was not in the right place, and the feeling of peace evaporated. I had come to the correct classroom on the wrong day. It turns out I didn't belong. Too embarrassed to say anything, I slunk out and never said a word to the TA. In a matter of minutes, I went from feeling *acknowledged* and *significant* to feeling *rejected* then completely *embarrassed*.

## Loved

    **v:** 1. to hold dear;
        2. to feel a lover's passion, tenderness, or devotion for;
        3. to like or desire actively: take pleasure in;
        4. to thrive in
    **The opposite of loved is scared.**

Love is the foundation for peace and, as we've discussed, the opposite of scared. Some people look at this placement and ask, "Aren't love and hate opposites?" We're bucking conventional wisdom on love because the goal of the Feeling Grid is to equip you to connect with yourself and with others.

When we talk about the emotion of love, the focus is on relationships rather than just objects and activities. In the English language, *love*, like *scared*, is a catch-all term that gets thrown about like confetti for any and everything we enjoy:

    I love roller coasters!
    I love pizza!

I love cake!

I love hiking!

I love _____ (fill in the blank)!

The truth is, as enjoyable as all those things are, those statements can't move people into a deep enough understanding of who we are in order to create real connection. On the Feeling Grid, the word love refers to *feeling* loved in relationship to and with other people. It isn't about romance, pleasure, infatuation, or physical passion. In the Feeling Grid, love depicts the kind of connection that encompasses many (if not all) of the feelings in the Peaceful Box. The Tier-Three words *encouraged* and *protected* offer further insight into what it means to feel loved. These are the actions of love.

## *Encouraged*

> **v:** 1. to inspire with courage, spirit, or hope: hearten;
> 2. to spur on: STIMULATE;
> 3. to give help or patronage to: FOSTER
>
> **The opposite of encouraged is discouraged.**

Do you feel encouraged by the people in your life? Do people feel encouraged by you? If so, that is a sign of feeling loved and of loving others. When people are in relationships where they feel discouraged—either by the other person's words or behavior—they experience fear rather than love and peace.

## *Protected*

> **v:** to cover or shield from exposure, injury, damage, or destruction: GUARD, DEFEND
>
> **The opposite of protected is exposed.**

Good parents love their children. Part of that love is shown through physical and emotional protection. The most basic example of love is providing clothing and shelter—in other words, protection from being exposed to the elements. We stand up quickly for the people we love. We demand that they are treated fairly or well. To the best of our ability, we ensure they have what they need to survive—even thrive—because we love them. In fact, shouldn't this be our goal with all people? We should want to protect all people who suffer and are exposed to abuse, torment, inequality, persecution, illness, and deficiency. This is protection! This is love!

## Secure

    **adj:** 1. free from danger;
          2. easy in mind: CONFIDENT

    **The opposite of secure is helpless.**

You may have assumed that *insecure* would be the opposite of secure. Perhaps there's an element of insecurity when you feel helpless, but the word insecure carries unnecessary and unhelpful baggage. It's an overused word that people tend to use in anger (rather than fear) as a criticism of themselves or others. Think of any 1980's movie featuring "Valley girls," and it's easy to picture one of them saying, "Oh my gosh, you're so insecure!" (That image alone was enough to make us leave insecure off the Feeling Grid.)

The opposite of helpless is *secure*. When we feel secure about ourselves, our relationships, our decisions, our jobs, or anything else, we have peace about those things. The Tier-Three emotions of *safe* and *trusted* relate directly to feeling secure. You may also notice how this emotion overlaps with feeling loved and assured.

**Example:** Have you ever found yourself on the highway behind a pickup truck with a load of furniture in it? If you were traveling behind this Eagle Scout, you could be confident that nothing would fly out and crash into your windshield. When I load furniture in the back of my truck, I use ropes and knots that keep everything securely in place. I do that for the other drivers' benefit and my own. I want to be able to drive peacefully. When I come up to someone using bungee cords to hold a

200-pound dresser that's bouncing all over the truck bed, that rubber band gives me no peace at all! You can bet I'm going to move toward peace as quickly as possible by passing that guy as soon as the coast is clear.

## Safe

> **adj:** 1. free from harm or risk;
> 2. secure from threat of danger, harm, or loss;
> 3. not likely to take risks: TRUSTWORTHY, RELIABLE
>
> **The opposite of safe is vulnerable.**

Safety is one of the five essentials of well-being in the workplace, according to guidelines from the US Surgeon General.[13] Safety can refer to literal physical safety in terms of machinery and job site conditions. Or it can refer to mental and emotional safety in terms of harassment, belittling, or threats of firing. Feeling safe allows you to focus on your work. Feeling safe in other relationships is equally important.

## Trusted

> **v:** 1. to rely on the truthfulness or accuracy of: BELIEVE;
> 2. permitted to stay or go to something without fear or misgiving
>
> **The opposite of trusted is useless.**

Trust is intertwined with feeling safe and secure. If your boss has everyone walking on eggshells because you never know when she's going to explode in anger and fire someone (picture Miranda Priestly, portrayed by Meryl Streep in *The Devil Wears Prada*), you feel a serious lack of trust in the relationship. The only thing that is predictable is that at some point, someone will be fired—and you don't want it to be you! That kind of emotionally unsafe work environment contributes to gossip and other behaviors that may make your coworkers seem untrustworthy as well.

When you think about the opposite of trusted, useless, picture that wonky bridge we mentioned under the definition of *secure*. If you don't trust the bridge's construction and are unwilling to cross it, it is useless to you as a means of getting to the other side of the river.

## Assured

**adj:** 1. characterized by certainty: GUARANTEED;
2. very confident: SELF-SATISFIED

**The opposite of assured is dread.**

When you *know* without any doubt that you are loved in a relationship, you feel secure, content, and *assured* that you can trust that person to not just accept you but also support you. That assurance gives you a sense of peace.

When you experience *dread*, it's because you expect (*know* or *believe*) something bad or unwanted to happen. The desire or need to control circumstances or outcomes can reveal a lack of assurance. Trying to control the situation or attempting to plan for and eliminate any surprises can be a person's way of seeking the assurance (and peace) they desire.

## *Relieved*

**adj:** experiencing or showing of *relief* from anxiety or pent-up emotions.

***Relief:* n:** removal or lightening of something oppressive, painful, or distressing

**The opposite of relieved is surprised.**

I started Chapter 6, "Fear," by sharing the story about losing James at the hotel in Corpus Christi. The intense relief I felt when I saw him with Susan and knew he was okay was a welcome change from the dread and helplessness I'd felt only seconds earlier.

On a lighter note, the surprise of unexpected visitors can change with the relief that they finally leave.

## Certain

**adj:** 1. fixed, settled;
2. dependable, reliable;
3. inevitable

**The opposite of certain is apprehensive.**

If you are apprehensive about taking a shortcut to the airport, you will feel more peace with the certainty of your familiar route. Being certain, whether it is of an outcome or your standing in a relationship, provides a sense of peace that comes from knowing what to expect.

## Content

**adj:** feeling or showing satisfaction with one's possessions, status, or situation

**The opposite of content is anxious.**

Contentment is what Goldilocks was looking for—porridge that wasn't too hot or cold, a chair that wasn't too big or small, a bed that wasn't too hard or soft. When things were "just right," she could finally rest. This peaceful emotion denotes satisfaction that brings an end to striving and allows you to simply enjoy the moment. Although it's adjacent to apathy in the Fear Box, it's important to remember the carefreeness of contentment is not due to lack of care but, instead, to satisfaction. In this I-want-more culture we live in, it's important to recognize and relish contentment.

## Relaxed

**adj:** 1. freed from or lacking in precision or stringency;
2. set or being at rest or at ease;
3. somewhat loose fitting and usually casual in style

**The opposite of relaxed is overwhelmed.**

Relaxed is one of the words that does not need a big introduction. Most everyone knows what relaxed means, but knowing what relaxes you is the goal. What relaxes you? This isn't a flippant or rhetorical question. You might struggle more than you expect answering this question. I choose to get therapeutic massages at our local physical therapist office. We run long distances, and this provides tension release in all my muscles! Susan, on the other hand, enjoys the dentist. She appreciates the guilt-free time of unavailability. So, for both of us, as different as our stress-free destinations are, we are both achieving a relaxed state of mind. The opposite of no responsibilities is too many responsibilities, and this is where the opposite of relaxed comes in, feeling overwhelmed.

## Satisfied

**adj:** 1. pleased or content with what has been experienced or received;
2. paid in full

**The opposite of satisfied is worried.**

If you are satisfied, you are content. If you feel worried, you don't feel satisfied with the potential outcome of a situation. You lack assurance or certainty that things will go the way you want. The worry goes away when the situation is satisfactorily resolved or when you shift your attention to another emotion.

# GET EMOTIONAL

Finding peace is like solving a long algebraic equation. You have to show your work so you know where you are messing up when you realize you are not feeling peaceful. This is similar to when you are uncomfortable and realize it. We want you to stay in that uncomfortable and find those missing steps that got you there.

When are you the most uncomfortable? What leads to that discomfort? Go back in time and narrow down your two most uncomfortable moments. I suggest these moments be in your adulthood years, as opposed to seventh-grade English class. But, if that's where you need to go, that's okay. Use the left side of the Feeling Grid to describe those feelings of uncomfortableness. Now, use those same feeling words to find the opposite of what you were feeling when uncomfortable. If you were feeling rejected, then you will focus on the feeling word accepted (on the opposite side of the grid). If you were feeling avoidant, then you will focus on the feeling word aware.

## Going Deeper

- What feelings are the opposite of the uncomfortable feeling in your peace equation? What has helped, or could help, you attain those feelings?

- Were you able to identify the specific feelings of uncomfortableness in the moment?

- Were you able to recognize the opposite feeling words on the other side of the Feeling Grid that correspond?

- What is it about the opposites (joy, peace, empowered) that resonate with you? How can you attain them?

# Peace
## Captured in a Quote

"I believe that every single event in life happens in an opportunity to choose love over fear."
—*Oprah Winfrey*

"When the power of love overcomes the love of power, the world will know peace."
—*Jimi Hendrix*

"Peace is not something you wish for. It is something you make, something you are, something you do, and something you give away."
—*Robert Fulghum*

"All you need is love."
—*The Beatles*

"Trust is the antidote that overcomes fear—and fear is the greatest inhibitor of all to a relationship that welcomes and nurtures new ideas."
—*John Pepper*

# Empowered

Using power detains while feeling empowered sustains.
—*Susan Duncan*

**THE ULTIMATE TREATMENT GOAL FOR OUR CLIENTS IS TO FEEL EMPOWERED.** Theoretically, we would define the goal for our clients in therapy as self-actualization. Carl Rogers (person-centered therapy) defines self-actualization as a continuous lifelong process that focuses on maintaining the individual's self-concept through reflection and reinterpretation of the individual's experiences, which promotes recovery, change, and development throughout life.[14] While this is part of the theory Bryan and I work from in therapy, we view the feeling of *empowered* as the emotional version of self-actualizing. Reflecting on your emotion helps you become emotionally aware of yourself. Empowered is only experienced when you practice emotional awareness and allow time in sadness and fear, as well as seeking joy and working for peace.

Isabel, our daughter, has always had to work at speaking up for herself. I tried to bribe her to walk up to the counter at Dairy Queen and order a second ice cream treat. She just stared at me like I was crazy. Granted, she was five years old, but I could already tell she was going to need some coaching out of her introverted little self. I even bribed her with the idea that she could have two ice cream treats. Nope, not happening.

Fourteen years later, she ran out of rubber bands for her braces, and her orthodontist was two hours away, so I suggested calling a local orthodontist to help her make it until her next appointment. She sent me a picture of her new rubber band package through text, also stating, "That was so uncomfortable, but I did it!" I asked her if it was hard to do, and she responded, "I kind of liked it; weird, eh?"

No, it's empowered, and that's not weird at all.

One of my best friends Greg, an amazing trial attorney from Alabama, taught me to always ask the question. It never hurts to ask, but it sure can be scary learning how to do it when you are uncomfortable or nervous. I thought of what Greg had taught me and sent Isabel a text wondering if she would get it: "It is kind of empowering, isn't it?" Her response: "Yes!" Isabel made the decision to call; she didn't let her fear overtake her, and she was able to attain her goals based on what she decided internally. Calling didn't make her feel empowered; she felt it beforehand. Calling and surviving the call solidified her feelings of validation, confidence, and worthiness.

Isabel was aware of her fear of being uncomfortable when talking on the phone and even more aware of calling a stranger who had no reason to respond in kind. She was ready to put herself out there. Recognizing and understanding her fears was what helped her find empowerment in her situation. The rubber bands were not the goal; the goal was Isabel feeling as though she could speak up and ask a stranger a question.

We teach and push practicing emotional awareness because it's the only way to attain the goal of feeling *empowered*. You have to know yourself in order to connect with yourself emotionally, as well as connect emotionally with others. Think about it this way: If you want to learn

Spanish but don't practice or study it, are you going to understand it if someone comes and speaks Spanish to you? No, you have to practice the language. Empowered is a feeling that, like joy and peace, comes from within—but it is dependent upon your ability to recognize the feelings of joy and peace.

Spending time with yourself builds awareness, approval, strength, importance, respect, and worthiness. When you share your feelings with others, which we have established as something that can be difficult to do, you have reinforced these same empowered feelings.

## FILL YOUR CUP

Have you ever had to use one of those short slightly-tiered Styrofoam cups outdoors? I remember using those little cups at picnics or birthday parties at the park as a kid. If you did not drink all of the contents, you could set it down with *confidence*. But as soon as you drank enough brightly colored punch to create a less-than-half-full cup of liquid, the slightest breeze would sweep it off the tree stump or picnic table and send it somersaulting across the grass, leaving you without a cup.

You are like that little Styrofoam cup. If you fill it with external things, there is a likely chance these things will go away, and your cup will be empty. If you fill it with internal things, your cup will never blow away. What you put into this cup drives whether you will experience feelings of awareness, intimacy, strong, important, respected, and worthy. Or possibly confident, secure, cared about, or admired.

What do you fill your cup with? If it is what others think of you, whether your children will come to visit, or if you get noticed at work, it will eventually blow away.

I created this metaphor after working with my client; let's call her Jody. Her presenting problems were that her best friend had let her down, her son did not show up for her, and her husband didn't talk to her. She felt worthless.

Jody would come to session and share her joy and excitement when her children were all at her house for Christmas and when her family invited her over for family gatherings. Then, she would come to session and be completely depleted and sad because nobody was talking to her, her friend ignored her, and she was not allowed to have her grandson for a holiday. I would notice she would be full of confidence or full of criticism and blame others for making her sad.

I said to her one day, "You are like that little Styrofoam cup—you know, the one that flies away the minute you drink too much of the contents?" She just stared at me.

"It's time to build up your confidence," I said. "That way, when the external doesn't show up and people let you down, you don't lose yourself." I suggested we work on her emotional awareness and spend time in the areas of seeking joy and working for peace to fill the bottom of her little Styrofoam cup because when family lets her down, she needs something to hold onto—herself. Family members' and close friends' decisions are external. Emotional awareness of self is internal.

Fast forward two years, and she started her session with, "I am doing okay. My birthday was last Monday, and it was okay. I wish my whole family would have come to celebrate my big 7-0, but they didn't. My son is not doing well, and my mom is still mad at me, but I am all right. Is that okay to feel all right even when they are struggling and not showing up for me?" I actually felt goosebumps. I was so excited for Jody. Feeling *all right* was amazing! In my head, I heard the guy on the Spanish channel announcing a goal in the soccer game—GOOOOOOOOOOOOOOAAAAAL!!! Then, I calmed down and got back to the therapeutic feedback.

I smiled and said, "Look at that little Styrofoam cup holding its own in a windstorm."

It's absolutely okay! She had filled her own cup by validating and valuing herself. For Jody, it took two years of hard work, reflecting, changing, and growing emotionally aware of herself. Feeling okay while others were not doing well in Jody's life did not diminish anyone else's worth. It simply meant she wasn't solely dependent on others to feel important and strong.

So how do you fill your cup? By not expecting external things or people to make you feel better and instead relying on yourself to feel okay where you are, even if where you are at the moment is uncomfortable. It's recognizing your fear or sadness and then working through those emotions that enables you to develop the kind of joy and peace that no one can take from you.

Learning how you feel and connecting with others through emotions allows you to become who you are, which enables you to experience feeling empowered. While empowered is the goal, it is important to understand that, like every emotion, it ebbs and flows. You will not feel 100 percent confident or respected all the time, every day. In fact, people whose answer to "How are you doing?" is consistently "I am great!" make me uneasy. When (not if) anger, fear, or sadness arise, don't be surprised and don't beat yourself up. Acknowledge the emotion, and then work toward the emotion you *want* to feel. That's how you live *empowered*.

> *Acknowledge the emotion, and then work toward the emotion you want to feel. That's how you live **empowered**.*

## FACING YOUR FEARS IN THE ABSENCE OF ANGER

"So something happened with my wife that I still can't believe," Martin said. He leaned forward to tell the story. "She came into the kitchen and asked me to help with her computer because it was freezing every time she opened a document.

"I get nervous when she asks for help because we usually blow up at each other. So this time, instead of following her back to the office to look at the computer, I told her I could help, but there were three things she needed to do to get the computer ready for me. If she would do those three things, I could keep the document from freezing." Martin shook his head and continued. "Well, she called my name a few minutes later, and I walked into her office and looked at the computer. I started to sigh loudly and was immediately aware that I was getting angry, but then realized this was because I was getting scared of her soon-to-be reaction. So I calmed my tone down and told my wife I could not help her until she did the three things I'd asked her to do.

"She nearly blew a gasket and started yelling about never being able to get her stuff done. I walked out, simply backed out of the room, and went back to the kitchen. I was stirring my coffee when I heard her walk into the room. She said that she was ready for my help. I nearly dropped my coffee cup when she told me she had done the three things I had asked. I got up and walked back to her office, sat down, opened the document, and showed her how to keep it from freezing. Then I got up, and she sat down without a word. Just as I walked out of the room, she said, 'Thank you.'"

Martin's smile was one of complete joy, as well as surprise. He sat back, took off his glasses, and lifted them slightly in the air and shrugged, "Can you believe that?"

I (Susan) was so caught up in his story that I had to recalibrate back into therapeutic mode. I asked one of my favorite questions, "What did it feel like to not get angry and, on top of that, watch your wife stay calm, and even thank you?"

Pushing the framed Feeling Grid sitting on the coffee table in front of Martin toward him, I asked him to find the feelings that helped him describe his experience.

He looked first at the Joyful Box and listed *appreciated (opposite is betrayed), free (opposite is guilt),* and *pleased (opposite is grief)*. I asked if he felt peaceful. He moved to the feeling words in the Peaceful Box, and he listed *acknowledged* (opposite is inadequate), *significant (opposite is insignificant), accepted (opposite is rejected),* and *supported (opposite is concerned)*. Then, without me asking, Martin moved his finger toward the Empowered Box and pointed to *respected (opposite is hateful), important (opposite is selfish), strong (opposite is mad), validated (opposite is jealous),* and *confident (opposite is envious)*.

None of the empowered feelings Martin identified were feelings he was used to. His underlying problem in counseling was years of PTSD caused by experiences in the line of duty. He was a seventy-three-year-old man who had been battling panic attacks and high levels of anxiety since he was twenty-six years old. When he felt anxious or uncertain about what might happen in a volatile moment with his wife, he would react with anger. All the feelings of fear and anger that he had experienced in battle would rush in and overwhelm him in those moments. He had been married for more than forty years, but he spent the last ten years working to not be angry at his wife because getting a divorce was too expensive.

More than anything, Martin feared getting angry and losing control. By walking out of the room instead of reacting in fear or anger, he proved to himself that he was in control of his emotions in that moment. That is empowering! His show of strength came from within. He did not have to react in anger to try and protect himself.

Martin's ability to choose to not react in anger came from being self-aware enough to recognize that it wasn't actually anger he felt; he was fearful of getting into an argument and losing control. Instead, he stayed who he wanted to be in the moment, which was calm. He chose to walk away until the tension had cooled. His empowered response had an impact on his wife as well. She, too, chose to calm down, realizing, perhaps, that she was frustrated with the computer, not her husband, who legitimately wanted to help her.

He could see the argument coming, and he had a choice. He could have used power (anger) to control the situation. Instead, he chose to deal with the moment differently and due to spending time becoming more self-aware of his emotions, he was able to feel empowered in the moment. The feelings of peace and joy that coexisted in that empowered moment were far different from what he was used to feeling. Typically, he felt anger followed by sadness (guilt, shamed, despair) and fear (rejection, helpless, anxiety). Throughout the next year of therapy, this one experience of feeling empowered is what helped Martin experience more moments of feeling empowered. Importantly, his wife began to feel more confident in the relationship, and the whole basis of their marriage shifted to connecting more emotionally as a couple. They have even moved into couples counseling! Just like anger begets anger, empowered begets empowered.

## POWER VS. EMPOWERED

*Power* was the word on the original Feeling Wheel, but when Bryan developed the Feeling Grid, we chose the term *empowered*. During our early writings with emotion, it was (and still is) a heightened time of sensitivity with gender, sexism, and the #metoo movement. Using the word *Power* in connection with feeling Successful, Respected, and Aware did not sit well with me. I imagined sitting across from a husband and wife in a session and asking either of them if they had attained power in the marriage. *Power*, especially when it comes to relationships, does not sound positive, healthy, or loving. And, after reading this book and spending time with your emotion, we think you will agree that the term power does not fit anywhere in any relationship.

Empowered is the *opposite* of Anger in the Feeling Grid. The term Power is actually more aligned with Anger. If that sounds like we are arguing semantics, remember that it is the nuances of words and using the right words to describe our feelings that make the Feeling Grid work so beautifully. Knowing the difference between these two words will help.

One of Bryan's favorite tactics in therapy is to define words in the moment, especially as a client uses them. So I looked up the definition of empowered and power in the Merriam-Webster dictionary.

## Empowered

**n:** having the knowledge, confidence, means, or ability to do things or make decisions for oneself

## Power

**n:** possession of control, authority, or influence over others

Based on these definitions, empowered is internal, and power is external. Let's use the first word listed in Tier Two of Empowered as an example: *aware*. When you are aware, you are at ease. Let's say you are going on a blind date. Knowing more about the person gives you the ability to be present in the moment before your date shows up.

My client Courtney was an only child. Courtney's mom was sixteen when Courtney was born. Her mom dealt with her feelings about having a child at such a young age by trying to control every aspect of Courtney's life. The power Courtney's mom exerted over Courtney's life was rooted in fear. As a result, Courtney developed anxiety from always being told what to do but also never knowing what to expect. She was told to come visit her parents every weekend, but when she arrived, she would not know what they wanted from her. She would bring her dogs and get reprimanded for bringing them, and then she would not bring her dogs and get reprimanded for being irresponsible because she left them at home. Her parents maintained control over her living environment and expenses, and they planned her vacations to ensure she spent time with them. Courtney was thirty-eight years old!

Over time, Courtney grew to hate being around her parents. Even at thirty-eight, she felt guilty when she disagreed or argued with her mom or dad. She had lived her whole life following their directions and living by their rules, and she felt like her parents still had power over every aspect of her life.

"What is it you want from them?" I asked Courtney one day during her counseling session. "What is one thing that you think could help your visits to their house?"

She sat for a good two or three minutes (That's a long time to be silent in a counseling session!), then she looked at me and said, "I just want to be aware of what I am getting into each time I visit them."

We had spent the first thirty minutes of her session talking about how she avoids talking to them about her relationship with them. She saw her visits with them as basically putting in her time while staying with them.

Look for Avoidant on the Feeling Grid. You'll find it in the Anger Box, which is where Courtney had been living for far too long. The opposite of avoidant is aware. It took several sessions to understand how she was operating emotionally with her mom and dad, and avoidant is where we started; then she moved into feeling sad because she loved her parents and did not want to avoid them. Once she became more emotionally aware of herself while spending time with her parents, feeling empowered began with Courtney simply wanting to become aware. Becoming aware is a great place to begin the journey toward feeling empowered.

## EMPOWERED: HOW DO YOU FIND IT?

We began this journey by introducing anger. From there, we worked our way out of anger into sadness and fear, the underlying feelings that instigate reactions full of anger. Understanding and recognizing emotions of sadness and fear is what moves us toward joy and peace. As peace and joy occur more frequently, feelings of empowerment begin to surface and resonate. The more peace and joy in your life, the more empowered you feel.

> *The more peace and joy in your life, the more empowered you feel.*

When a client experiences feelings of empowerment, Bryan and I don't stand up, pump our fists in the air, and say, "Yes! You are done! You're empowered! You never have to talk about emotions again!" Remember, feeling empowered ebbs and flows, just like all the other emotions. But you will experience the feelings of empowerment more often than before. The more self-aware you are, the easier it will be to move fluidly from feeling to feeling. You are better able to anticipate possible emotions because you have felt them before. Empowered is a nice emotion to add to your "Emotions Résumé."

We've said this before, and it bears repeating here: Emotions are moments. They come and go—and you can feel more than one at a time. Empowered can encompass joy and peace, or it may be accompanied by only one of those feelings. Empowered can even share space with sadness or fear. What empowered cannot share space with is anger.

Clients do not usually seek counseling *because* they feel empowered. No one calls to book an appointment, saying, "I am doing very well, feeling confident, respected, loved, and accepted. How do I keep it going?" That would be great! But no, clients come to counseling due to the lack of these feelings. They want to feel joyful, peaceful, and empowered, but they don't know how to get there. Most of the time, they don't have the words to express how they feel or what emotions they are seeking. They just know they want to make the "bad" feelings go away.

When clients don't have words to express their feelings, we start by looking at how their emotions are showing up—their external expressions of emotion. We usually begin by looking at the Anger Box. Why?

- Because anger is a more culturally acceptable reaction than fear or sadness.

- Because denying, ignoring, or suppressing fear or sadness often leads to anger reactions.

- Because anger is an instinctive, protective reaction. We all feel it. It's what we do when we notice its presence that matters.

- Because anger creates more anger. It never solves the problem or truly resolves the issue.

The more you employ anger to cover fear and sadness in your life, the less connected you will feel—to *anyone*—especially yourself. That's a huge problem when connection is what humans need most to feel emotionally strong and healthy. Thus, anger doesn't work.

As we stated at the very beginning of this book, people who lack emotional awareness and connection often turn into *Angerballs*. They clam up, lash out, or store up resentment—*and spread anger everywhere they go*. When clients review angry feelings in the Feeling Grid, they find a plethora of words to describe what they are feeling: avoidant, defensive, mad, selfish, hateful, disgust, and more. Having identified what they're feeling, they can move across the Feeling Grid to see what empowered emotions are missing from their lives. When people see the words in the Empowered Box, words like *accepted, worthy, important, validated, respected,* or *successful,* they know that's how they want to feel.

While anger is the most commonly used feeling, empowered is the most difficult to identify—even when you're experiencing it. That's due, at least in part, to the fact that most people don't stop to notice what they are feeling when things are going well. Just as Bryan didn't notice at first that what he felt on those camping trips was peace, we rarely slow down and describe what we are experiencing when we feel positive and lighthearted. We simply feel it.

Recognizing the moments you are exhibiting joy, peace, or both and sharing those feelings with others allows them to grow. The same is true when it comes to feeling empowered. We'll close out this chapter by defining the empowered feelings. Pay attention and notice when and where these emotions show up in your life. When feelings of joy, peace, *and* empowerment become familiar, you will notice them more readily. You'll even learn to find them in the midst of fear and sadness.

## CONCLUSION

You finally made it to the end of your emotional language lesson! Your work is done. Let the bliss begin. Well, not exactly. Now you are entering the maintenance of relating and connecting. All of the emotions on the grid will continue. Yes, even anger will be something to monitor. The important part is to continue to use and work through the Feeling Grid.

When you get mad, you need to recognize that you are using something that doesn't work. Not only that, but you are also likely covering up some form of sadness or fear. By the way, this also applies when you hear someone else's anger directed toward you. You have to be authentic about what you are feeling. Is it sadness? Is it fear? Pick the one that resonates most, then try to become more specific. Identify the Tier-Two emotion next. Which Tier-Three emotion fits best in this moment? Identify any overlap in the feelings above and below. Now you are really pinpointing where you are emotionally.

If you are willing to acknowledge and share these feelings, then you are moving across the grid. That's right—you are either seeking joy or working for peace. Now what? This is the nice part. Just as much as we naturally or habitually gravitate away from our feelings of sadness and fear toward anger, we do the same with empowered. Feeling joy and peace creates a natural movement toward feeling empowered.

Empowered does not require that you seek it or work for it directly. It just happens. The seeking and working take place as you move from sadness and fear over to joy and peace. But that empowerment will only be for a moment and for the situation in which it occurs. You will have to repeat these steps for different situations and relationships and with different experiences. The more this becomes your habit, the more easily empowered is achieved as connections continue to maintain in your life.

# EMPOWERED EMOTIONS

| TIER 3 | TIER 2 | |
|---|---|---|
| Present / Close | Aware | EMPOWERED |
| Connected / Caring | Intimate | |
| Patient / Gentle | Strong | |
| Validated / Confident | Important | |
| Gracious / Faithful | Respected | |
| Deserving / Admired | Worthy | |

## Aware

**adj:** having or showing realization, perception, or knowledge

**The opposite of aware is avoidant.**

Avoidant is an anger reaction that gets in the way of our progress toward joy or peace. When we choose to be aware of what we are feeling—both our struggles as well as joy and peace—we experience empowerment in the smallest degree. With awareness, we can be more empowered to make changes, build relationships, or end relationships if necessary.

Taking time to look at how much anger you use on a daily or weekly basis is a simple exercise that makes you more aware of your actions, interactions, and behaviors. G.I. Joe always said, "Knowing is half the battle." It's true! Awareness is a powerful first step for moving toward what you want to experience and for connecting with others. In fact, not using avoidance and simply identifying your feelings in either sadness or fear is awareness. That is empowering.

The Tier-Three emotions of Aware offer an interesting dichotomy in that it is possible to be present without being close and vice versa.

## *Present*

>**adj:** 1. now existing or in progress;
>    2. being in view or at hand

>**The opposite of present is detached.**

You can be in the room without being present. Maybe you're on your phone, answering work emails while you are at your child's basketball game. Your body is in the stands, but even from the court, your child knows you aren't really there. Or maybe you're at dinner with your spouse but fail to hear a word they're saying because your thoughts are consumed by the realization that you need to talk with your aging but fiercely independent father about the fact that he really shouldn't be driving. Checking emails and planning for your family's future is not wrong, but if it keeps you from attaching emotionally to the person in front of you, then you are not present.

Being present physically but not emotionally is a power move, one in which you detach from others. The result of this disconnection in the relationship is likely to be an anger reaction. That's because your emotionally disengaged presence can be hurtful; in fact, several clients have commented that the parent who was around but never engaged caused more feelings of hurt than the parent who was never there.

Now imagine being fully present at that basketball game and making eye contact when your son makes a three-pointer. Your son is empowered by your noticing, praising, and appreciating him, and you are empowered by his response to your presence. If you are going to be present, commit to being fully present.

## Close

**adj:** 1. being near in time, space, effect, or degree;
2. familiar

**The opposite of close is distant.**

Closeness can be related to physical presence certainly. That sweaty, excited hug after your kid's basketball game may put you a little closer physically than you want to be, but the emotional closeness you share as you celebrate that moment together is just right.

Emotional connection isn't confined to proximity. You can be in Texas and still be close to your child, who is away at college, or to your brother, who lives six states away. Closeness is developed through familiarity, which comes from sharing experiences, thoughts, and emotions. You can do that face-to-face or miles apart, but you can't be close without being authentic.

## Intimate

**adj:** 1. marked by a warm friendship developing through long association;
2. of a personal or private nature;
3. marked by very close association, contact, or familiarity;
4. INTRINSIC: ESSENTIAL

**The opposite of intimate is defensive.**

Intimate is a powerful internal experience that bolsters empowered feelings. Unfortunately, the word is often misused as a synonym for sex or for the name of the ladies' undergarments department in stores. (It's funny that men's underwear is not called *intimates*, but that's a topic for another book!)

The definitions above, however, offer something deeper than sex and underwear. Intimate is feeling close and familiar. It is developed through relationship. It is personal and, like emotional connection, it is intrinsic or essential to who we are as humans. Intimate denotes a feeling that is more powerful than being vulnerable with someone. Although there is a connection between these words, vulnerable carries a feeling of fear. Knowing yourself intimately is empowering. Knowing someone else can be intimate. Maybe the empowering feeling of being intimate comes from our movement through our fear and vulnerability. Experiencing true intimacy in a relationship happens when we have approval and a connection with that person that allows us to be authentic.

## *Connected*

**adj:** joined or linked together

**The opposite of connected is sarcastic.**

With the underlying theme of emotional connection, *connected* is a word we have used frequently in this book. But connected is also a simple feeling word. For defining and understanding the feeling word connected, let's keep it simple. Do you know yourself better and connect with your emotions when they occur? Do you feel connected to your children? Do you feel connected to your parent, best friend, or coworker?

Connected does not have to mean married or committed. Connected refers to having an idea of what you are feeling or what the person you are talking to in the moment is feeling. What creates this connection? As you have moved through all the other feelings in the Feeling Grid, connecting is about listening for feeling words. When you hear them, you connect.

Bryan and I listen for feeling words in session, from the intake session to the session of termination. I listen for feeling words everywhere. As soon as I hear a feeling word, I am much more at ease in knowing where the other person is (You Are Here), and I have a better idea of how to be there for them. Feeling words connect people—*if* people listen for them.

## *Caring*

**adj:** feeling or showing concern for or kindness to others

**The opposite of caring is exasperated.**

Caring was the very last word added to the Feeling Grid. Again, filling and defining the right side of the grid was the most difficult part of the development phase. Caring showed up in session quite a bit. Clients would ask, "Where is caring? I feel like I am caring," or "Why can't she just care about me?" Caring didn't make it on the early versions of the Feeling Grid because we also needed the words around it to relate. As we came to the end of writing this book, we realized that caring is related to feeling intimate, connected, and patient. It is the opposite of exasperated.

There is nothing more personal and connecting than telling someone that you care about them or feeling how much someone cares about you. To care about someone is empowering—you are free from hiding any emotion and not afraid of exposing your true feelings.

I remember sitting in the interview for my doctorate program in front of a panel of faculty members. The last question was, "Where do you see yourself in ten years? What will you have accomplished?" Many interviewees stated goals of writing books, becoming public speakers, and providing research that would help change the field of psychology. I was getting exasperated every time I heard another response because mine had nothing to do with research or writing books (which I find kind of funny to recall as I write this book). I was afraid my answer wouldn't be accepted, but I stayed true to my goals.

"I just really want to help people. I want to be an excellent clinician to help clients and meet them where they are struggling," I responded confidently. Sharing that I cared about my future clients' needs was empowering.

## Strong

**adj:** 1. having or marked by great power;
3. having great resources

**The opposite of strong is mad.**

The culture we live in promotes the idea that strength is displayed best by not feeling—which is, of course, impossible. Short of avoiding the basic emotions of sadness and fear altogether, the options are denying these feelings or overcoming them with brute force. Neither of these choices is helpful or empowering.

If you've learned anything from this book, we hope it is that true strength comes from acknowledging your emotions, especially the tough ones. Withholding thoughts and feelings doesn't make you strong. Avoidance is not a strength. Ignoring your feelings and just carrying on does not make you strong.

It takes strength to admit when you feel sad and seek comfort and joy. Confessing your fears is a courageous and strong move! And it is the only one that will empower you to find peace.

Being strong is an important feeling, an empowering feeling.

## *Patient*

**adj:** 1. bearing pains or trials calmly or without complaint;
2. manifesting forbearance under provocation or strain

**The opposite of patient is frustrated.**

If you are frustrated because you can't make a putt, open a jar of pickles, or figure out a math problem, you have not been successful at being patient. Maybe it's traffic, or your spouse not taking out the trash, or your friend is running late . . . again. These are all frustrating, and patience is hard to find. Frustrated seems to be the word that everyone is most comfortable admitting when it comes to their anger.

Imagine what your relationships would be like—what the world would be like—if *patient* was the feeling with which you and everyone else were most comfortable. There would be no frustration. We would be able to remove the horns from our vehicles, and waiting in line would never be a problem. What a world!

Being patient can transform not only how you feel but also how others interact with you. Being patient relieves you from needing to react, which is quite empowering.

**Example:** Susan and I went out to eat during a busy season in the college town where we live. We had a server who was flustered and greeted us late. She apologized and took our drink orders. Still appearing flustered a few minutes later, she apologized again. She was running late, but we were not bothered by it. We both had waited tables in college, so we were empathic to the job. We gently asked, "Are people frustrated with you right now and not treating you very well?"

She replied, "My worst day ever. I've already made a few mistakes, and it's going to be a bad day!" We assured her that we understood, had nowhere to be, and that we could be patient as she got caught up.

Our patience helped. It was empowering for her—and for us. We were free from finding fault with her, fault in others, and sat back and enjoyed the moment. Our server seemed to calm down and didn't apologize profusely anymore. I think she felt some peace as she waited on us. Being patient sounds easy, but it's not. It takes practice, just like all the feelings we are introducing to you.

## *Gentle*

**adj:** 1. free from harshness, sternness, or violence;
2. SOFT: delicate;
3. MODERATE;
4. KIND: AMIABLE

**The opposite of gentle is furious.**

At first glance, gentle and strong seem like they could be opposites. It takes true strength, however, to be gentle. Gentle is the epitome of self-control. In the face of fury, we need gentleness—from us and toward us.

Some of the strongest people I (Bryan) know are parents of children with special needs. They exhibit an abundance of gentleness, and it takes a lot of strength. I'm sure that, at times, they may feel moments of fury or frustration. What I admire most is these parents' willingness to connect with and draw support from others by acknowledging their feelings of fear and sadness. It's their awareness and strength that brings them right to patience and gentleness.

## Important

**adj:** marked by or indicative of significant worth or consequence: valuable in content or relationship

**The opposite of important is selfish.**

Curt Smith and Roland Orzabal from Tears for Fears put it best: "Everybody wants to rule the world." Everyone wants to feel important. We want to matter to the world or at least to our little corner of it.

It's perfectly fine to be confident—to know your self-worth. It's even okay to want to be recognized or appreciated for your efforts, talents, and contributions to others. Experiencing empowerment, joy, and peace in connection to this feeling of importance happens within the bounds of two caveats:

1. Others can't be the only source of validation. We've already discussed how important it is for you to be able to fill your own cup. External recognition feels great, but don't rely on it to satisfy your need for importance.

2. Your sense of self-worth (confidence or importance) can't overshadow or over*power* others' needs. Remember the difference between power and empowerment. The opposite of important is

selfish, a kind of self-importance that may breed an envious desire for what isn't yours or anger that shows up as jealousy as you seek to protect what you have.

## *Validated*

>**v:** 2a. to support or corroborate on a sound or authoritative basis;
>2b. to recognize, establish, or illustrate the worthiness or legitimacy of
>
>**The opposite of validated is jealous.**

Take a moment to imagine yourself feeling the following things all at the same time: secure, accepted, encouraged, noticed, appreciated, and proud. It would be amazing to have those feelings, especially all at once. Now, let's add some context. You are feeling all those feelings at your workplace after a promotion. That is validating! Imagine all those feelings on your wedding day as you hear the vows being shared with you. That is validating! Imagine you just read your letter of acceptance into college. That is validating!

Validation can help us to feel important, but it is something to recognize that this important and validating feeling comes from feelings of peace and joy. We gravitate toward empowerment when we have feelings of joy and peace.

## *Confident*

>**adj:** 1. full of conviction;
>2. having or showing assurance and self-reliance
>
>**The opposite of confident is envious.**

You can feel validated without feeling confident, but when you accept validation and *own* it, you experience confidence. Where validation might be about a specific idea or accomplishment, confidence comes from within and develops from knowing that your self-worth is not based on what others think, do, or say. That means 1) You can feel confident even without external validation, and 2) envy is not an issue.

## Respected

>**v:** considered worthy or high regard: ESTEEM
>
>**The opposite of respected is hateful.**

Hate shows little to no respect and is a tool of power. Respect is a tool that equips the empowered, and it comes from joy and peace. Respecting yourself allows you to live from a state of confidence where you feel certain of your worth, regardless of others' opinions or actions.

For me (Bryan), the Tier-Three feelings of *gracious* and *faithful* capture two attributes that I respect most in others.

## *Gracious*

>**adj:** 1. marked by kindness and courtesy;
>    2. MERCIFUL
>
>**The opposite of gracious is resentment.**

Gracious people demonstrate respect. Respecting others empowers them to respond with grace (kindness or courtesy) even when they disagree with or dislike someone. They refuse to let misgivings rule their lives because the joy and peace they experience from within frees them from resentment or holding past wrongs against others or themselves. Gracious is the epitome of forgiveness.

If you really want to work on forgiveness, you must also understand resentment. The definition of forgiveness is to stop reacting in anger or feeling resentment. Forgiveness does not mean to stop feeling sad or stop feeling afraid. It simply means that you stop being angry. Applying grace in your life for yourself and for others can become one of the most empowering parts of your life. That is the challenge. If you are thinking you can go straight from mad to forgiving, that is too challenging. You have to move through the Feeling Grid to get there.

## *Faithful*
**adj:** steadfast in affection or allegiance

**The opposite of faithful is irritated.**

Faithful seems like another strange "emotion" to be placed on the Feeling Grid. Holding our ground and being reliable to our values, friends, family, business partner, God, or spouse can become very empowering. It is a challenge to move past the irritating and annoying things that might interfere in our lives, but when we hold fast to what we value, we share more about our character. This is who we are as a person. This is faith in ourselves and where we put our faith: God, family, or wherever this emotion falls in our lives.

The term faith is somewhat synonymous with going in blind. Isn't it empowering to be able to walk into a moment blind because you trust yourself and how you will be in the moment—no matter what externally is happening? Faith begets empowerment!

## Worthy
**adj:** having worth or value

**The opposite of worthy is disgust.**

Susan's podcast cohost showed up one day wearing a T-shirt that read, "I'm rooting for all the good people."

Susan's immediate question was, "Only the good people, really?" This begged the follow-up question: Who gets to decide who's *good* enough for a cheering section? Who is worthy?

The answer: You are. We believe wholeheartedly that every single person has inherent worth and value, not just the "good" ones. We believe *you* have worth and value, and we are rooting for *you*.

But it's not what we believe about you that matters.

On the Feeling Grid, when we talk about worth, we are talking about how you feel about yourself. Our hope is that as you seek joy and find peace, you will experience the empowered feeling that comes from understanding your worth. And if you don't feel worthy, know this: That feeling, too, can change.

Carl Rogers, one of the founders of humanistic psychology, espoused the belief that there are three tenets that are "necessary and sufficient for change":[15]

1. Empathy
2. Warmth and genuineness
3. Unconditional positive regard

I hold to these tenets closely. To regard others as having value is a positive and empowering thing. When you practice empathy toward yourself, are kind to and honest with yourself, and hold yourself in "unconditional positive regard," in time, you will discover the truth: You are worthy.

## Deserving

**adj:** having good qualities that deserve praise, support, etc.: MERITORIOUS

**The opposite of deserving is appalled.**

*Deserving*, an external expression of worthy, sits opposite *appalled* on the Feeling Grid. Imagine someone who is appalled—*disgusted*—with something or someone, saying, "Well, that is unacceptable! I won't allow it!" That appalled person will stand in opposition to whatever or whomever he or she is disgusted by.

That's what people do to themselves when they feel undeserving. They sabotage themselves by giving up right before the finish line (or even before they get to the starting line). They pick fights in relationships, not because they dislike or are even upset with the other person, but because they feel unworthy of that person's love or attention. Certain they will be rejected, will fall off the wagon, or won't make the cut, they hand over any potential for joy and peace to shame and worry.

So what does deserving look like? It looks like a willingness to try again when the tough conversation didn't go well the first time. Someone who feels deserving will say, "Okay, I messed up, but I can start again right now," and then they do because they have hope for a better future. Someone who is empowered knows they deserve to be treated with respect and that it is okay to ask for support when they need it.

## *Admired*

**v:** 1. to feel respect and approval for;
2. liked very much

**The opposite of admired is critical.**

We don't criticize things or people we admire. We appreciate them for what they are—and we let them know it. At the same time, we don't expect them to be something they aren't.

It is easier to admire others than to admire ourselves; in fact, the idea of admiring yourself sounds a little like the evil queen in *Snow White* saying, "Magic Mirror on the wall, who's the fairest one of all?" But you don't have to go that far (or be weird and evil) to feel admired. You just have to acknowledge that you are worthy of admiration.

Maybe you've known someone who deflects every compliment. Or maybe you are that person. The next time someone says, "Great job!" or "You look great!" or "That was delicious!" remember that you are worthy of admiration and say, "Thank you."

# GET EMOTIONAL

Feeling empowered is the goal! Who does not want to feel validated, important, present, respected, or worthy? But the important part is to not aim for empowerment. If you are pursuing empowerment as your goal, you will typically find yourself on the opposite side, demanding validation, importance, closeness, respect, and worth. In fact, the goal is still to work through the Feeling Grid. Empowerment comes through joy and peace, so that is where we look.

In order to feel empowered, you must recognize the feelings you experience on the way to feeling empowered as you pass through sad, fear, joy, and peace. For this exercise, choose the four empowered feelings that you identify with the most. Once you have identified these four feelings from the Empowered Box, list what feeling words in Joy and Peace resonate with your four feeling words from the Empowered Box. Now, look at the feeling words opposite of all the feelings you chose in the Empowered Box and the Joy and Peace Boxes. Do the opposite words resonate with where you get stuck?

| Empowered Feelings | Joy | Peace | Sad | Fear | Anger |
|---|---|---|---|---|---|
| 1 | | | | | |
| 2 | | | | | |
| 3 | | | | | |
| 4 | | | | | |

## Going Deeper

- What led you to choose the four Empowered feelings words in column one?

- What led you to connect your choices of Joy feelings with the Empowered feelings in column one?

- What led you to connect your choices of Peace feelings with the Empowered feelings in column one?

- Do you resonate with the opposite feelings of Joy and Peace that present in Sad and Fear? Are these feelings typical of your struggle?

- Are the Anger feelings that are opposite of your Empowered feelings your typical reaction? How are they different?

# Empowered
## Captured in a Quote

"To err is human; to forgive is divine."
—Alexander Pope

"To lose patience is to lose the battle."
—Mahatma Gandhi

"Respect is one of life's great treasures. I mean, what does it all add up to if you don't have that?
—Marilyn Monroe

"Without feelings of respect, what is there to distinguish men from beasts?"
—Confucius

"I was always looking outside myself for strength and confidence, but it comes from within. It is there all the time."
—Anna Freud

# What Now?

**EMOTION ENCAPSULATES ALL ASPECTS OF OUR LIVES.** We feel all the time. It's only 9:18 a.m. as I work on these closing thoughts about why Susan and I wrote this book and what we hope you'll take away from it, and already today I have experienced at least seven different emotions! Some feelings come and then pass in an instant. Others hang around awhile. Becoming aware of our feelings, particularly those that have an impact on our thoughts, conversations, decisions, and actions, is crucial to our relationships.

Emotion is what fuels our ability to relate to others and to understand ourselves. It is not just a means of connecting—it is the only way to truly (authentically) connect with another human being. Can you get along in life without understanding what you are feeling or without intentionally and honestly connecting through emotion?

Yes. You can choose not to acknowledge your emotions. You can put on blinders and pretend that you don't notice someone else mad or sad or scared. We all do it. That's why the world is full of *Angerballs*. One anger reaction leads to another, and before you know it, you're angry all the time because you're sad, afraid, or lonely and can't tell anyone about it.

That's no way to live.

Listen, we're not saying that emotional connection is easy. It isn't. First, you have to acknowledge what you're *really* feeling, and then you have to share it. If you've read this far, you know we're not going to let you off the hook by only using the socially acceptable words like *frustrated* or *mad* or *irritated* and leaving it at that. Identifying those anger reactions is a place to start. To get to *empowered*, however, you have to do the real work—the hard work—of spending time with yourself and identifying the underlying emotion.

---

*To get to empowered you have to do the real work—the hard work—of spending time with yourself and identifying the underlying emotion.*

---

You are not alone in thinking that this whole open, authentic, reality-driven, non-avoiding practice of emotional expression is difficult. Emotional expression is hard for me, too, and I talk about emotions for a living! When thrust into a situation where connection means that I need to explain (not hide) how I feel, I generally stumble to find a clear response or to quickly understand myself in the moment. If I have a copy of the Feeling Grid handy (either on paper or one of the pillows that Susan gave me for Christmas), I grab it and search for the right word.

My own practice of emotional expression and connection is a work in progress. I keep at it, though, because I know it works. I see the impact in our clients' lives, in our family, and in my own life.

In learning the language of emotion, you are embarking on something challenging. Don't give up this pursuit. Notice how you feel and use your emotion to connect. Discovering how to move from anger, sadness, or fear into joy and peace is empowering and so worth the effort.

## Just be.

You have learned how to recognize your feelings of anger, sadness, fear, joy, peace, and empowerment. With a better handle on how emotions function in relationships, you might be thinking: *Now what?* Now that you are aware of all these emotions, what do you do with them? The answer is simple: You don't have to *do* anything. The purpose of this book is to find ways to *be* . . .

Be aware of how you are reacting.

Be aware of what you are feeling.

Be intentional about understanding what you need.

Be brave enough to share what you're feeling in the moment—or after the fact if you need a few moments to think about it.

Be okay with being uncomfortable, whether that means fully experiencing sadness or admitting to feeling fear.

Be realistic and know that simply identifying what you are feeling doesn't make sadness, fear, or anger instantly go away.

Be empowered in the knowledge that joy and peace come from within, which means they are within reach.

Just be in your emotions.

## Share what you feel.

The simple truth is that trying to be anything different from what you feel simply isn't real. Radio host and storyteller Brant Hansen said, "No amount of sincerity can change your reality."

Reality—real life—is where the challenge starts and continues. You must be willing to experience your emotions, know your emotions, and share your emotions. That does not mean that you must cry all the time or hug everyone you see. It does mean you cannot deny or ignore how you feel.

What you share may vary within your various relationships. For spouses, children, and parents, it is probably great to share more and often. With strangers, I still try to connect through emotion, but I don't give all the details. That's me. You may get into a conversation with a stranger and share more openly. That's fine.

## Let emotion empower you.

Emotions will not be the basis for all decision-making, but they must be included. Just because I am afraid of an activity does not mean I should let my fear dictate what I do. Being empowered by emotion, rather than controlled by it, means that I must determine whether my fear is serving or sabotaging me. I let my fear inform my decision-making, but I weigh the options and try to look at life from different angles. I may even ask someone I trust to help me think through a decision that my fear is trying to block.

If you have been hurt in relationships in the past, romantic or otherwise, knowing your hurt allows you to protect yourself from relationships with people who behave in a similar way. Your awareness may allow you to end potentially hurtful relationships. If you have a relationship, like so many, that involves hurt and love, but you don't want it to end, let your awareness empower you to navigate the relationship. You can choose to respect yourself by setting boundaries, for example, rather than falling into anger. Acknowledging feelings of shame and rejection equips you to work on the relationship and develop trust.

## CONNECT WITH EMOTION.

Emotions are the vehicle for our connection, and they must be a part of our process of relating. Ignoring your feelings may create resentment or confusion, but rarely (if ever) will it bring about a positive outcome.

I have a recent client who has been married for fifty years. He has been avoidant of all feelings for the entirety of his marriage. Having retired, he suddenly had more time with his wife. She wanted to connect, but he didn't know how. Both of them have contributed to the communication struggle that left them feeling lonely and confused. Not connecting only created greater discontent in their relationship.

Connecting with emotions is a two-sided adventure, meaning you need to seek to understand others' emotions. If you have struggled to find, understand, and share your emotions, you can bet that the people around you may have similar difficulties. They may, for example, say that everything is fine, which leaves you with no idea about what is really going on for them. Sometimes, your willingness to share your emotions can inspire others to open up. Other times, they may hesitate, unsure of how to communicate in a new way.

I had a client who was tired of his corporate job and wanted to find something different, something fun that allowed him to enjoy his work. He shared with his wife how he felt. He expressed his feelings of sadness, despair, and loneliness, as well as the dread and helplessness he felt in his job. His wife responded by saying, "No!" and very little else. He talked about this encounter with me during a session and said he felt rejected by her and sad about not being understood.

I asked him how she felt. Her "No!" that I pointed out might seem like a location on the emotional map, but it did not give him any real information about where she was emotionally. To get anywhere in the relationship together, he needed to understand how she felt.

The purpose of exploring her emotions was not to convince her or change her mind but so they could know each other and how their decisions impacted each other. This information did not immediately solve the problem, but it put them on a level where they could work together.

Being emotional changes the landscape of how we relate as individuals, couples, businesses, corporations, governments, and society. This is the power that rests in being able to relate more fully. We don't believe that all problems and struggles go away because people are using more emotion. We know it is bigger than that. We also believe, however, that the struggles and difficulties we do have will diminish when we are more connected. As you grow more connected to yourself, your spouse, your children, your parents, God, employers, employees, friends, and even the occasional stranger in the grocery store, you are nurturing a network of connection that can continuously help you through your struggles, problems, and difficulties.

Be emotional.

Be connected.

Be empowered.

# APPENDIX

The following are a few truths we wanted to share that didn't fit elsewhere in the book.

## EMOTIONS ARE *NOT* DISORDERS.

The Feeling Grid is intended to help you identify the feelings you have in the moments you experience them. The Feeling Grid is not something that you superimpose with something like mental health disorders. If you are talking about phobias or mood disorders like depression and even a history of trauma, then you are looking at a disorder that has other symptoms that might include some emotional responses, but the emotion is not the defining part of this issue. It is important to remember that feelings are moments. You might feel sad with major depression. You could feel scared with a specific phobia. You can feel apprehensive in post-traumatic stress. You can also feel all of those feelings without any of them being related to a specific mental health disorder.

As a therapist, I tend to look at presenting concerns for individuals based on their relationships. It is the lens in which I view most areas of mental health. If this is the case, then emotions and connection are going to be the most important factor in relating. Just because you struggle with emotions and relating does not mean you have a mental disorder. But your ability to relate might still be a problem for you in your relationships.

## IGNORANCE IS NOT BLISS.

This is the phrase we use to explain away our not knowing as something useful. I get that we can maybe find some peace in not knowing things, like what is in that hot dog. We can just enjoy the taste of the hot dog. But not knowing about ourselves is not happiness. Not knowing what others are thinking and feeling is not bliss. Not knowing leaves you disconnected.

A large portion of our caseload is working with the geriatric population. In many cases, individuals present with the challenges of transition in their lives, but they also run into some problems with connection. They are discovering, only now, that maybe they are not connected to their spouse, their children, or especially themselves. The focus they have applied throughout their life is to not connect with their emotions. The best way to think about this is that ignorance is avoidance.

You might argue that they were happy at one point. They stopped working, and then things changed, and that is what they are unhappy about. That might be true, but we are talking about relationships. If your focus has been on avoiding this emotional communication, then you will certainly and assuredly run into issues of distance in your relationship. You can continue to blame others for being the ones who changed, but that is exactly the point. You never adapted and connected. This leaves you struggling with sadness and fear in a whole new way.

I want to warn you: It might seem easy in the moment to not deal with what you feel. You might even forget about it for a time. The danger comes when you are older, and the people that you are closest to no longer want to have a relationship with you. You are left alone. It will be much harder later in life to make these changes and build connections.

Your ignorance is not others' problem to solve. It is yours. The good news is that you can learn this way of relating. Men, women, children, adults, young, old, and across so many cultures, emotional connection is possible. It is time to put aside your ignorance and pursue the connections you crave.

## EMOTION RERUN

I'm totally making up this term, but this is an important part of moving through the Feeling Grid. Emotion Rerun is when you or someone you know uses the same feeling to describe their experience in multiple settings and situations. They might exclaim that their feelings are hurt all of the time. It becomes a pattern of communicating that becomes frustrating for the person who is hurt, but it is also frustrating for the people trying to connect.

Let's begin with the person committing the rerun. The reason this is likely frustrating is that you are using a word/emotion that you are familiar with, and you are stuck using this word. Continuing to explain your emotion as "hurt" when this is not the actual feeling—or not really specific about what is happening—has no choice but to be frustrating. You are trying to explain something about yourself with the wrong emotion. Every bit of comfort you are requesting is geared toward your hurt. But if that is not the actual problem, then you are going to be dissatisfied with all their efforts. You have to expand your emotional repertoire and not use the same old emotion for every scenario and situation.

Explaining and developing your use of the full Feeling Grid will help avoid Emotion Rerun. You want those needs met, and the best way is to give accurate information. If you don't, this is the same as trying to measure your weight with a thermometer. The answer will not be accurate at all.

Emotion Rerun becomes frustrating for the people who are hearing your same emotion as well. It becomes frustrating for them because they are trying to accommodate that feeling, but they never seem to satisfy or comfort that feeling. That is because it is the wrong solution. They appear to be addressing the hurt, but they keep being told that you are hurt.

You continue to feel hurt despite all of their efforts. Maybe hurt is not exactly what is happening. Perhaps your pain could be better explained by expressing rejection. Feeling insignificant has a different solution from being disappointed. Plus, it is about addressing fear rather than sadness.

## WHAT IS NOT ON THE FEELING GRID

There are occasions when I run into words or phrases that have become known as feelings and yet are not going to be on the Feeling Grid. We are introducing these now because you may have noticed their absence, or you might run into these phrases as you begin to open up and share. We will explain these "pseudo-emotions" and the dangers of using them. Predominantly, you will find that these words do not provide clarity or specificity to what you are feeling. Thus, it becomes difficult to connect with these feelings.

### "I'm fine" is a lie.

You have heard this line so many times. You may have a tone that you have associated with this comment. It's possible for me to see a smile with this statement. I have also experienced hesitancy with this statement. On some occasions, I have experienced downright hostility. This is where we get some confusion in emotions. If one statement can mean so many different things, then it is not going to be useful in helping others connect.

The truth is that this statement comes from one of several places. We either want everything to be fine, or we are trying to make sure that we are meeting others' expectations that everything is fine. We are not able to specify what we are feeling. The lack of specificity in what we feel is a struggle to help others know where we are emotionally. Fine is not a word that you can find on the Feeling Grid because it is not an emotion. It does not capture with specificity how you might feel in a way that others can connect. If you are happy, state that you are happy. If you are content, then you should say content.

The first reason people might use this expression is because they have the expectation that everything will be joyful or peaceful. If you are angry at your friend and just exclaim, "I'm fine," when you are obviously not, there is a clear expectation that you want to be where you are not. You are struggling with the sadness or fear that is happening, and you are delving into anger. You are avoiding dealing with your feelings and not seeking joy. You might exclaim that nothing is wrong, but you are trying desperately to be okay. This is the wrong approach. It lacks authenticity of your emotions when you might feel sad or fear. We might be angry, and we are not talking about this struggle with being angry in the situation.

The next reason we use this expression is that we believe others expect us to be fine. We believe and state nothing can be wrong with us because people don't want to know what we are feeling or care about what we are feeling. Again, we have the wrong assumption here. We are trying to deal with what we think may be happening with others but never really addressing what is going on for ourselves. "Fine" lacks connection, and this is why it is not on the Feeling Grid.

## "I'm upset" is a setup.

The antithesis to feeling *fine* is upset—another word we purposefully left off the Feeling Grid due to its lack of specificity and connection to others. This phrase might work a little differently from fine, but it has the same outcome: no connection.

So many people use upset because they describe themselves or others this way. I have been guilty on recent occasions of using this phrase, but here is the problem. I don't know what upset means. The definition states that upset is being forced out of the usual upright, level, or proper position. A turtle on its back is upset. People are not upset. And people using upset do not provide understanding.

Is upset about our sadness, anger, or fear? It could be all three. Since using such a general word like upset provides no merit, we did not include this word in the Feeling Grid. You would be advised to stay away from this phrase as well.

What makes this phrase so bad? The biggest issue with not having specificity is that you cannot look to the other side of the grid to find what someone needs. It sets up the possibility of confusion, disconnect, and anger. You will feel lost, and eventually, those needs will not be met, and you can move to greater amounts of anger being expressed. That is what we don't want. If you say "upset," then look for a different word. If you hear someone say "upset," explore with them more deeply whether the struggle is in sadness or fear.

## *Hangry* is not an emotion or an excuse.

This word is totally made up. Okay, I've been guilty of making up a few things here, but mine has sound reason. The idea of being hangry, a combination of anger set on by hunger, does not work for this grid.

I can begin with the fact that hungry is not a feeling. It is a sensation, generally an unpleasant one, but hunger is not an emotion. The emotion is our reaction or response to being hungry. So we want to separate sensations, beliefs, ideas, and thoughts from being considered purely emotional.

The other important factor is that you are angry out of hunger. Well, that's just childish. So are most of the anger words and responses. You are essentially not getting what you want, and because of that, you are letting people know about it—loudly. This is not a reason to be angry or use anger. Anger does not work!

# BIBLIOGRAPHY

1. "CDC's Developmental Milestones." *Centers for Disease Control and Prevention.* https://www.cdc.gov/ncbddd/actearly/milestones/index.html.

2. Wilcox, Dr. Gloria. "The Feeling Wheel: A Tool for Expanding Awareness of Emotions and Increasing Spontaneity and Intimacy." *Transactional Awareness Journal* 12, no. 4 (October 1982), 274–276, DOI: 10.1177/036215378201200411.

3. Gottlieb, Lori. *Maybe You Should Talk to Someone: A Therapist, HER Therapist, and Our Lives Revealed.* New York: Houghton Mifflin, 2019.

4. Thompson, Curt. *The Soul of Shame: Retelling the Stories We Believe About Ourselves.* Westmont, IL: InterVarsity Press, 2015.

5. De Bont, Jan, director. *Speed.* United States: Twentieth Century Fox, 1994.

6. Yalom, Irvin D. *The Theory and Practice of Group Psychotherapy, Fourth Edition.* New York: Basic Books, 1995.

7. Rogers, Carl R. *On Becoming a Person.* Boston, MA: Houghton Mifflin,1961.

8. Eckman, Paul. "Basic Emotions." In *Handbook of Cognition and Emotion,* edited by T. Dalgleish & M. J. Power, 45–60. New York: John Wiley & Sons Ltd., 1999. https://doi.org/10.1002/0470013494.ch3.

9. Cameron, Julia. *The Artist's Way, Anniversary Edition.* New York: TarcherPerigee, 2016.

10. Briggs, Jean L. *Never in Anger: Portrait of an Eskimo Family.* Boston: Harvard University Press, 1971.

11. Anspaugh, David, director. *Rudy.* United States: TriStar Pictures, 1993. 1 hr., 54 min.

12. Dunlap, Keith. "Rip up the Winning Ticket? Five Reasons Why Winning Lottery Can Destroy Lives." *Nwes7Jax.com,* July 14, 2023. https://www.news4jax.com/features/2023/01/12/rip-up-the-winning-ticket-5-reasons-why-winning-lottery-can-destroy-lives.

13. Athitakis, Mark. "Study: Toxic Workplaces Remain a Challenge." *Associations Now,* August 15, 2023. https://associationsnow.com/2023/08/study-toxic-workplaces-remain-a-challenge.

14. Rogers, Carl R. *Client-centered Therapy: Its Current Practice, Implications and Theory.* London, UK: Constable, 1951.

15. Rogers, Carl R. "The Necessary and Sufficient Conditions of Therapeutic Personality Change." *Journal of Consulting Psychology* 21, no.2 (1957), 95–103. https://doi.org/10.1037/h0045357.

# THE MARRIAGE KNOT

**Marriage is hard.** It's a lifelong commitment and a mysterious endeavor that people jump into everyday untrained and ill-prepared. When challenges inevitably arise, tempers flare and anger becomes the emotional reaction of choice.

Drs. Susan and Bryan Duncan developed the Marriage Knot using their theory of emotional connection and the Feeling Grid. By improving emotional intelligence and communication, the Marriage Knot equips couples with the tools to share authentic feelings and demystify the marriage relationship.

Although the Marriage Knot was designed as an intensive to help couples in crisis, the material is beneficial for all marriage relationships as it teaches spouses how to manage struggles with less anger—because struggles will happen. The key is learning how to use tools like the Feeling Grid, Romantic vs. Reality, and Psychobiology of Love to uncover the real issues and find a path toward healing.

If you are contemplating divorce, dealing with anger, arguments, or extramarital affairs, or are experiencing intense disconnection and loneliness in your marriage, the Marriage Knot offers you the tools and hope to find healing and recovery for your marriage.

# God has a plan for your marriage.
## The Marriage Knot will help you rediscover how good life can be together.

### THE MARRIAGE KNOT INTENSIVE WEEKEND

This weekend-long intensive gives couples the chance to get away from everyday stressors. With more than twenty hours of guided instruction in a safe, neutral environment, you'll learn strategies and techniques to shift out of old habits. As you discover healthy ways to fight for your marriage, you'll establish new behaviors and communication skills.

### *THE MARRIAGE KNOT* BOOK

Coming soon, *The Marriage Knot* book makes these powerful tools and strategies more accessible than ever before. Whether you've been married for four months, forty years, or you just got engaged, *The Marriage Knot* will empower you to build a stronger healthier relationship with your spouse.

Learn more at
knowtheknot.com

# About the Authors

BRYAN DUNCAN, PhD, is a psychologist and the clinical director and owner of DA Counseling. After completing his doctorate in counseling psychology at Texas A&M University, Bryan worked in college counseling centers at Appalachian State University and Texas Tech University before moving into private practice. He has worked with clients in juvenile justice centers, long-term care facilities, school districts, and courtrooms. With more than two decades of counseling experience in a variety of settings, Bryan has worked with couples, families, groups, and individuals, including children, teens, adults, and seniors. His experience with such a diverse client base has convinced him that it is never too late to repair or strengthen relationships and that the key to doing so is understanding and sharing emotions.

Bryan and his wife, Susan, established their private practice, DA Counseling, in 2011. Today, they live in College Station, Texas, where he enjoys spending time with his family, and pursuing his hobbies of long-distance running, cooking, and camping.

**SUSAN DUNCAN, PhD, LPC,** is the executive director of DA Counseling and lecturer at Sam Houston State University. In addition to seeing clients at their private practice, Susan and Bryan co-lead Marriage Knot intensives, working to help couples restore their relationships through improving emotional connection and communication.

After earning her master's degree in clinical psychology and doctorate in research, measurement, and statistics (Educational Psychology), she discovered a love for teaching and helping students find confidence in their studies. Throughout her career, Susan has been an assistant professor and lecturer while pursuing independent statistics research and consulting. When she isn't seeing clients or teaching, Susan loves hanging out with her family and enjoys traveling, running, and camping.

www.ingramcontent.com/pod-product-compliance
Lightning Source LLC
Chambersburg PA
CBHW061811070526
44586CB00024B/2808